Linear Unit Grammar

Studies in Corpus Linguistics

SCL focuses on the use of corpora throughout language study, the development of a quantitative approach to linguistics, the design and use of new tools for processing language texts, and the theoretical implications of a data-rich discipline.

General Editor
Elena Tognini-Bonelli

Consulting Editor
Wolfgang Teubert

Advisory Board

Michael Barlow
University of Auckland

Robert de Beaugrande
Università del Litorale, Capodistria

Douglas Biber
North Arizona University

Chris Butler
University of Wales, Swansea

Sylviane Granger
University of Louvain

M. A. K. Halliday
University of Sydney

Susan Hunston
University of Birmingham

Stig Johansson
Oslo University

Graeme Kennedy
Victoria University of Wellington

Geoffrey Leech
University of Lancaster

Anna Mauranen
University of Helsinki

Ute Römer
University of Hannover

John Sinclair
The Tuscan Word Centre

Piet van Sterkenburg
Institute for Dutch Lexicology, Leiden

Jan Svartvik
University of Lund

John Swales
University of Michigan

H-Z. Yang
Jiao Tong University, Shanghai

Volume 25

Linear Unit Grammar: Integrating speech and writing
by John McH. Sinclair and Anna Mauranen

Linear Unit Grammar

Integrating speech and writing

John McH. Sinclair
Tuscan Word Centre

Anna Mauranen
University of Helsinki

John Benjamins Publishing Company
Amsterdam / Philadelphia

The paper used in this publication meets the minimum requirements of American National Standard for Information Sciences – Permanence of Paper for Printed Library Materials, ANSI z39.48-1984.

Cover illustration from original painting *Random Order* by Lorenzo Pezzatini, Florence, 1996.

Library of Congress Cataloging-in-Publication Data

John McH. Sinclair
    Linear unit grammar : Integrating speech and writing / John McH. Sinclair and Anna Mauranen.
    p. cm. (Studies in Corpus Linguistics, ISSN 1388–0373 ; v. 25)
    Includes bibliographical references and indexes.
    1. Grammar, Comparative and general.

    P151.S667 2006
415--dc22   2006051041
ISBN 90 272 2298 3 (Hb; alk. paper)
ISBN 90 272 2299 1 (Pb; alk. paper)

© 2006 – John Benjamins B.V.
No part of this book may be reproduced in any form, by print, photoprint, microfilm, or any other means, without written permission from the publisher.

John Benjamins Publishing Co. · P.O. Box 36224 · 1020 ME Amsterdam · The Netherlands
John Benjamins North America · P.O. Box 27519 · Philadelphia PA 19118-0519 · USA

Table of contents

Dedication	VII
Acknowledgements	IX
Preamble	XI
Introduction	XV

SECTION A Preliminaries

CHAPTER 1	Setting the scene	3
CHAPTER 2	Background	23
CHAPTER 3	Data description	41

SECTION B Analysis

CHAPTER 4	System of analysis	49
CHAPTER 5	Step 1: Provisional Unit Boundaries	55
CHAPTER 6	Step 2: Types of chunks	59
CHAPTER 7	Step 3: Types of organisational elements	71
CHAPTER 8	Step 4: Types of increments to shared experience	79
CHAPTER 9	Step 5: Synthesis	91

SECTION C Theory and follow-up

CHAPTER 10	The example texts analysed	107
CHAPTER 11	Theoretical synopsis	129
CHAPTER 12	Looking ahead	145

Appendix	167
Bibliography	175
Index of names	181
Index of subjects	183

In Memoriam David Brazil 1925–1995

The influence of David Brazil's subtle and innovative thinking will be found in many places in this book, not only where we specifically cite him. For twenty years he led generations of students at The University of Birmingham to find their own feet in his chosen domains of language teaching, discourse intonation and, latterly, syntagmatic grammar. He died just after his last book, *A Grammar of Speech* was published, and before he could actively promote the refreshing novelty of his view of text as a series of increments rather than sentences. As we developed Linear Unit Grammar we felt ourselves moving ever closer to David's position, and we hope that this book may serve to rekindle interest in David's work.

For more about the life and work of David Brazil see:
http://www.speechinaction.net/SPARC_Brazil.htm

Acknowledgements

Our thanks are due to the many colleagues who helped this project by their participation in the two workshops that we conducted, at Jaio Tong University in Shanghai in October 2003 and in Ann Arbor, Michigan in May 2005. Special thanks go to Professors Yang Hui-Zhong and John Swales respectively for their congenial hosting of the events, and to ICAME/AAACL for including the second workshop in the programme of their annual conference.

We owe a debt of gratitude to all those involved in making the data available to us. Most of those whose conversations are transcribed remain by convention anonymous, but public-spirited none the less. The offer of a sample from the Hong Kong Corpus of Spoken English came at a crucial point in our work, and we were encouraged by the interest shown by Professors Martin Warren and Winnie Cheng throughout the last year of the project.

Preamble

You are encouraged to work through the following introductory activity as a preliminary to the presentation of Linear Unit Grammar. Please look at Figure 1.

<blockquote>
theheadmasterofharrowtellsannmcferranwhyhehasl
etthetvcamerasintoaschoolfullofodditiesbarnabylen
on30thheadmasterofharrowschoolleansoverhisdesk
therearemoreimportantthingsinlifethanstrawboaters
</blockquote>

Figure 1.

We expect that before you are consciously aware of having thought about what Figure 1 is, you will have formulated a number of hypotheses about it and will have decided on a number of tactics for dealing with it, and will be first of all aware of the preliminary results of all this involuntary activity. It is a written verbal communication. There are traces of English words in it. It is a string of characters without spaces or punctuation or even capital letters.

Perhaps almost immediately, given your linguistic training, competence in English and expectations of this book, you will guess that it is a piece of written English rendered solely as a sequence of characters. You are then able to formulate a stratagem for dealing with it, and you settle on the "traces of English words" that was one of your immediate reactions. You decide that you will attempt to turn it into a string of English words, and then see if it makes sense. Perhaps some investigation that you are conducting subliminally reports at this point that there are signs of coherent phrases here and there, strengthening your hypothesis.

Not everyone will respond in the same way to Figure 1, and we would be interested to hear from anyone who has a strikingly different experience. The two points that we hope most readers will agree on are (a) that most of your reaction is involuntary, and the hypotheses and strategies are formulated with little or no conscious intervention; (b) you begin, mentally, to add word spaces, capital letters and punctuation in order to make sense of the passage. There is no need to copy it out and add all these features, because once you have the idea it will become almost immediately readable. Occasionally you may have to backtrack or read a string of characters several times before the word spaces become obvious, because there are some specific difficulties in this passage—one of the reasons why it was chosen. The proper names are slightly unusual, there are some words and phrases that may not be familiar to many readers — like *straw boaters* at the end. You may not be aware of Harrow school, an old English school, where hats called straw boaters are, or were, worn in the summer. On the helpful side there are repetitions like *the headmaster of harrow* and a cliché, *there are more important things in life than*, which, once noticed, explains almost a fifth of the whole passage.

The passage begins easily, because the most frequent word in English, *the*, heads the text. *Headmaster* is recognisable; in English it can be written in three different ways, *head master, headmaster* and *head-master*, and with or without initial capitals. In the original of this passage, curiously, the two instances are spelt differently, as a single word and as two separate words. *Of* is the second commonest word in English, fairly easy to spot; *harrow* may not be readily recognised, but *tells* is clear enough, so *harrow* must be something you can be headmaster of. If you saw the word *arrow* there you would have to revise your guess or have an *h* left over. The same goes for the *s* following *tell*. Perhaps at first its role as the present singular inflection is not obvious, and *san* could be the start of a name; the run of consonants *nnmcf* is a little off-putting, and indeed the whole string until *why* is encountered may be a puzzle. The clue is that many Scottish family names begin with *mc* or *mac*, signifying "son of". *McFerran* or *Mcferran* are plausible names, though unfamiliar to the authors; the original text reads *mcferran* which is certainly short of at least an initial capital. The occasional inconsistencies in the original text show that users of a language encounter routinely the same kinds of problems that the reader of Figure 1 is faced with, though usually diluted with plenty of unproblematic text. Once Ann Mcferran has been identified, the rest falls into place, and the first line is all but deciphered, because *he* and *has* are easy to spot. The line break splits *let*, but with *the* following it can be reconstructed quickly. *TV* is almost universal, and supported by *cameras*. By now the decipherer can polish off *into a school full of* without much perplexity, but the last few characters in the line may need a moment; *oddities* is not a common word, and *Barnaby* is not a common name, nor is *Lenon* unless you award it a double *n* in the middle and think of the Beatles.

The beginning of line 3 is distracting unless Mr Lenon has been identified, but 30th need not detain us, and the next phrase has occurred before, here with the helpful word *school* following for those not so familiar with UK institutions. By now *leans over his desk* should be easy because, unconsciously, we have become trained in this medium even over such a short passage, and headmasters have desks anyway. The last line is a quote from Mr Lenon, which we have already construed. (This extract is the beginning of a piece in The Times of 10th June 2001).

The task of separating words in a piece of ordinary printed matter is an unfamiliar one for most readers, but one that we adapt to readily, presumably working out ad hoc tactics as we go along. The keys to efficient performance include:

(a) the ability to apply a hierarchical model to the linear string — in this case to postulate, correctly, that the passage consists of a string of word tokens, and that a placement of word boundaries will make the passage instantly legible and understandable.
(b) the ability to *prospect*, to look ahead for features that will help the interpretation of a difficult passage or settle a question of alternatives
(c) the ability to hold provisional interpretations in mind and to abandon them if they are superseded by more plausible ones — otherwise to continue with them perhaps without resolution — like how exactly to spell *mcferran*.

In the rest of this book we will be applying essentially the same techniques to a later stage of the process of "making sense of" text. We will not artificially hamper ourselves as we have done in this illustrative exercise, but will use the same arguments, rely on similar perceptions, knowledge and abilities in the reader, and chart the progress of text from its fairly raw state in a range of situations to something that makes reasonably good sense.

Introduction

This book is the report of a study of language in use and how people manage it, handle it, cope with it and interpret it. The main focus is on informal spoken English, but the structural statements are intended to apply to all varieties of English, whether written or spoken, whether standard or non-standard, whether specialised or general.

This is an unusual and rather bold claim. Most descriptions concentrate on one language variety, whether they say so or not[1], and the descriptions often perform poorly with any variety other than the one chosen. The vast majority of grammars concentrate on the structure of carefully written English; discourse analysis concentrates on semi-formal spoken language, conversation analysis on informal and intimate spoken varieties. There are also studies of specialised varieties, but the texts studied fall within one or other of the major varieties just mentioned; the contrastive study of different varieties also keeps constant such parameters as spoken vs. written, formality and preparedness[2].

It is central to our position that all varieties of a language in use can be described using the same descriptive apparatus, in contrast to the present state of affairs, where grammars make little effort to be flexible. Linear Unit Grammar is a descriptive apparatus and method which aims at integrating all or most of the superficially different varieties of English; it does not attempt to replicate the kind of analysis that received grammars perform, but organises the text into tractable units for further analysis, whether conventional or any more innovative analysis. Its main function is to show step by step how a latent hierarchy can be discerned in the linear string of word forms.

The underlying hypothesis that guides this stage is that a person applies essentially the same creative/interpretive apparatus to any language text, rather than that we have to postulate the existence of more than one such apparatus.

The aim of reconciling different language varieties was not the original motivation of the study. Like any open-ended investigation, it had aims and objectives which were modified by interim results and by the experience of undertaking the research. To begin with, the project was little more than an informal probe search-

---

1. With some recent exceptions such as Biber (1988), Biber et al. (1999) and Carter and McCarthy (2006).
2. There are exceptions, of course, such as MICASE (http://www.hti.umich.edu/m/micase/), which has collected examples of academic spoken English from a wide range of encounters on the scale of formality.

ing for answers to three questions:

(a) Is it possible to divide running text into chunks by assuming, and calling on, speakers' perceptions about the divisibility of text?
(b) If so, do speakers divide up the same text in similar ways?
(c) If so, does the result of making the divisions provide a foundation for a meaningful analysis of text?

It became clear that the answers to all these questions tended towards the positive, and this feedback gave rise to further questions

(d) what role do chunks play in the analysis of text (i.e. the description of the way in which meaning can be systematically derived from text)?
(e) what range of text types can be naturally chunked?

The answer to (d) was along the lines of "central and pivotal in the early stages", and the answer to (e) was that apparently any text type could be chunked.

At this point a plan of campaign began to take shape. We had begun with a text which showed no boundaries except word spaces — the minimal transcript of an informal spoken conversation. Our approach to analysis through chunking allowed us to take the early steps without regard for the details of the internal structure of the chunks, so we could cope with texts that contained "irregularities" of many kinds without the system breaking down. In a conventional analysis it is often impossible to proceed at one level if the text manifests an unusual pattern at a more detailed level, because all statements in such grammars are mutually dependent. In contrast, our initial request to assign provisional unit boundaries did not require any explicit awareness of the internal structure of the chunks or their combinations — it was only the boundaries that were asked for.

We realised that this property of our approach made it possible to investigate, or at least to begin an investigation into, texts and text types which were not normally amenable to structural description. One of us (Mauranen) had begun a long-term study of English as a Lingua Franca, and we found that a modified version of our original analytical system could make a satisfactory preliminary analysis of a lengthy sample of this variety, and also brought out distinctions between this and our first text which were intuitively satisfying (see Chapter 10).

The word "preliminary" above is important, because our analysis is not intended to reveal all the structural intricacies of the texts, but rather to bring out their similarities and differences in a systematic fashion, so that the output of our analysis should be close to an acceptable input into any of the established descriptive grammars. There is still a problem in the expectancy of the established grammars in that they do not tolerate even small divergences from their requirement of well-formedness, so we developed an extension into structural description that overlaps with normal categories but is slightly more generalised, and so allows relationships to be determined while the data representation is still heavily linear (see Chapter 12).

In this we returned to the same stratagem that we started with — to concentrate not on the item, the token, the word, but on the relationship, the spaces in between. The inherent power and simplicity of this stratagem was demonstrated by Coniam (1998) in his "boundary" program devised over ten years ago, but it has not been followed up in software development. There is an implied claim in this stage of our work that the job of analysis is made easier and more accurate by separating the identification of units from the classification of constituents. When a text is divided into coherent units, and within those units the basic structural relationships have been assigned, the job of relating the constituent items to classes should be much easier than starting from scratch. This is a similar strategy to a "bootstrap" operation in computing, where initially the system can only cope with superficial and unvarying entities, but passes through stages of ever-increasing sophistication. In our case, it is guided by coming ever closer to embodying the meaning.

We then decided on several further text exemplars. Because of the novelty of our analysis we had to choose brief extracts, but increased our range of variety. We asked a team of researchers in The Polytechnic University of Hong Kong who were building a corpus of local spoken English (HKCSE) to send us a transcript of their choice — but not to include the sound recording.

Around this time we began to consider how adaptable the emerging system of analysis might be with respect to written varieties of English, so we decided to select three short passages and apply the same procedure to them as we had used in the spoken transcripts. One started from an earlier, unsatisfactory attempt to describe "compressed" English (Sinclair 1988), the highly abbreviated language associated with some reference books, and in the present era, text messages; the second was a passage from a famous novel (Joyce 1922) where the author seemed to be writing a simulation of speech; finally we chose a piece of written English which was as representative of ordinary expository prose as we could find — an editorial from *The Independent* newspaper.

We were pleased to find that our system coped with these completely different texts with only minor adaptation, and that the comparisons that we made after analysis continued to be intuitively satisfying, so we decided that we should publish our results in order to get feedback from the academic community.

Existing grammars

From time to time we make reference to the prevailing state of grammatical knowledge, the aims of grammar construction and the styles of presentation of grammatical information in a wide range of influential publications. Usually the context is the contrast between our approach and the main lines of what has gone before. To make the contrasts, we do not usually need to pick out one or more specific examples of received, conventional, etc. grammars, but we just lump them together. While this is rough justice, since each of them, and each category of them, has its own position in the panoply, we need to make it constantly clear that it is not our intention to mount specific criticisms of them; simply to make contrasts.

On the whole we expect readers to have sufficient familiarity with existing grammars to appreciate that our references are general rather than vague. But here is a brief checklist of the features that characterise Linear Unit Grammar, and which are not prominent in any other grammars:

(a) the maintenance of linearity in the description wherever possible
(b) the syntagmatic orientation of the description (in contrast with the paradigmatic orientation of most grammars)
(c) the "bottom-up" approach to description, though mediated heavily by intuition from the very first step
(d) the cyclical, "bootstrap" style of analysis as against the description of sentences in a single pass through the grammar
(e) the acceptance of any alphanumeric string that has good reason to be considered an instance of English text (in contrast with the basis of most grammars on the written form of the language).

This checklist anticipates much of the book that is to come, but may be useful to keep in mind.

Structure of the book

The reader's very first experience of this approach will be, we hope, the Preamble. There, in a very small exercise, a taster for the kind of data and argument is offered. After this Introduction we turn to the book proper, which is organised into three sections.

The first section is entitled *Preliminaries*. Chapter 1 raises the main conceptual points that the argument relies on, and illustrates by one brief and one extended example the general principles of analysis. Chapter 2 traces the origins of these conceptual orientations in previous literature, and attempts to acknowledge the important influences on our thinking. The early part deals with previous grammatical research, later on it tackles key works in psychology, education and applied linguistics. Chapter 3 is a short account of the textual data that we chose to describe.

The second section, *Analysis*, goes through the analytic method, which we call

Linear Unit Grammar (LUG) on a step-by-step basis which is much more than a procedure. After an overview of the descriptive method in Chapter 4, there are five chapters each of which describes a step in the analytic process. Chapter 10 rounds off this section with a short commentary on the six example passages in the light of the descriptions.

The third section raises, in Chapter 11, matters of theory on a broader basis than hitherto, using the experience of analysis as a guide. Chapter 12 rounds off the book by considering some developments and applications that interest us. First it considers the consequences of continuing the LUG kind of description into the area of parsing, where it begins to offer alternatives to conventional grammars; then it assesses the possibilities for automation, and finally the implications for Applied Linguistics.

The book finishes with an Appendix which reports on one of the Workshops that shaped the book, which was generously hosted by ICAME/AACL at Ann Arbor in May 2005.

This book has been written jointly, and each part of it has been discussed extensively. The core of the book, the analyses, were constructed in a lengthy process mainly using e-mail. This required each of the authors to make an individual analysis, step by step, without knowledge of the other's decisions, and for the discrepancies to be resolved by exchanging documents, often many times, finally reaching conclusions at one of several meetings we were able to have despite the physical distance between Helsinki and Florence.

The responsibility, therefore, is fully shared, but it is normal in such a publication to indicate which of us initiated the drafts of the chapters. AM drafted Chapters 3, 6 and 8, the commentaries on *ELFA*, *HKCSE* and *Independent* texts in Chapter 10, and the Appendix. Chapter 2, placing the ideas in their cultural roots, and Chapter 12, the applications, were written half-in-half, while Chapter 9, the final step in analysis, was a completely joint effort. JS drafted the rest, i.e. the Preamble, Preface, Chapters 1, 4, 5, 7, the *Lexis*, *Gazetteer* and *Joyce* texts in Chapter 10, and Chapter 11.

Terms and concepts

This book contains detailed analysis and discussion of the structural detail of texts, and we have tried to keep novel terminology to a minimum, though some is inescapable. The three terms that distinguish the study are:

Linear Unit Grammar (LUG). This is the name we have chosen for this descriptive model. It is a grammar expressed as far as possible in a linear succession of units.

Provisional Unit Boundary (PUB). The first step in analysis is the division of the text into chunks, which we separate with boundaries and call them PUBs.

Linear Unit of Meaning (LUM). After the chunks are classified they are recombined into units, now directly meaningful, called LUMs.

We do not define a chunk because we are using it as a pre-theoretical term. But on several occasions in the explanations we discuss the notion of a chunk in order to be as clear as possible about how we are using the word.

So our first step in analysing a text is to divide it into alternating chunks and boundaries (*PUBs*). Then we classify the chunks, and call them *elements*. Then we combine the elements into finalised meaningful segments which we then call *LUMs*.

Other words like "segment", "fragment" are used informally from time to time when we do not want to be more specific (but note that our term for the MF element is *message fragment*). Throughout, we refer to places in our transcripts as *lines* with a number; this is for reference purposes only, and the numbering in each example is particular to the example in its particular place in our argument.

Throughout, we use *text* or *texts* irrespective of whether we are referring to transcripts of a spoken encounter or written documents. We require a single term to talk about all our data, and indeed any sequence of alphanumeric characters, with or without punctuation. It is also convenient to use a term which is heavily associated with written language even though we are mainly talking about spoken varieties; our data consists entirely of material in written form, and we deliberately do not invoke aspects of spoken performance, even if we have access to recordings, so that the reader can follow our arguments and decisions directly with the data.

The term *message* is one of our main structural labels, and we have considered and reconsidered the term, because the concept it labels is open to various interpretations, even misunderstandings, and needs careful definition. We want a simple and transparent term, but in this area all the available words are open to misunderstandings; *topic, subject, subject matter, shared knowledge, shared experience* — none of these is "safe". We decided to pick our way in this minefield rather than devise special terms which would not be readily accessible to the reader. With proper safeguards, most of the terms listed above can be used.

In the case of *message* there are two possible inferences that we want to avoid:

(a) a message element is not some meaning which is coded into speech or writing and then decoded by the listener or reader; its meaning is integral to the way in which it is expressed

(b) message elements are not the only carriers of meaning; meanings which depend on the circumstances of real-time interaction are not expressed in textual message units, and so in LUG are paraphrased in parallel descriptive notes.

Message elements combine into message units. A message unit is a coherent stretch of text whose meaning is interpreted according to the structural conventions of the language. Its purpose is to update the virtual world of shared experience of the participants in the spoken or written interaction by means of topic incrementation. For the notion of *increment* we rely on Brazil's (1995) work, explained in Chapter 2.

The shorthand labels for the analytical categories are named below:

O	organisational element
OI	interactive organisational element
OT	text-oriented organisational element
M	message-oriented element
MF	message fragment
M–	incomplete message unit
+M	completion of message unit
+M–	partial completion of message unit
MS	supplement to message unit
MA	adjustment to message unit
MR	revision to message unit

Note that each LUM contains one, and only one, M.

SECTION A

Preliminaries

CHAPTER 1

Setting the scene

The aim of this chapter is, first, to introduce the concepts that are frequently invoked and used in the method of description presented in the analytical part, Section B. Some have already been encountered in the Preamble and Introduction, and several are returned to in Section C, for more detailed examination.

Secondly, this chapter presents two brief spoken text transcripts and, in advance of setting up the descriptive apparatus, goes over them word by word to demonstrate how the issues arise that are then systematised in Section B.

Variety within a language

There are many varieties of a language, but only one core grammar. Many, perhaps most, students of language would accept this as a very cryptic but essentially accurate statement of the relation between language in the mind and language in the world. However, the statement is an act of faith rather than a scientific conclusion, because there are no clear accounts of how the great variety of usage is explained in a single coherent grammar. This book offers to bridge that gap by setting out a method of relating together the many varieties of current English.

It was pointed out in the Introduction that the descriptions made here include several extracts from transcribed spoken conversations, and they are all called *texts*. This name is used mainly for convenience but also because the extracts are all in alphanumeric form when we start work on them.

Variety of languages (and descriptions)

Our statements here are intended to be accurate for current English, and, while we cannot make guarantees, relevant to texts in many other human languages. The phenomenon of *chunking*, which is the starting point of the description, is probably not restricted to any language or group; the simple structures of conversation that we describe are probably replicated, with minor differences, in hundreds or thousands of languages. All languages share the central feature that their physical form is linear but their abstract structure is held to be hierarchical.

We also frequently refer to the state of grammars, published descriptions and theories of language, and again our focus is on current English. Linguistic theories should be valid for all languages, but the available grammars, dictionaries and other resources differ a lot from language to language. Our comments refer to the situation for English, which as a language is probably the best supported by descriptive activity; nevertheless there is a lot of innovation in language description at present, and some recent grammars of languages other than English may be more advanced in relation to the matters discussed here.

Spoken and written variety

Language variety is usually subdivided in the first instance between spoken and written modes, and newcomers to language science face something close to a paradoxical situation; on the one hand the spoken form of the language is extolled as the primary form, the earlier of the two and the one where all the basic features were established; on the other hand it is the written form of the language that is described in almost all the grammars. True, there have been occasional nods in the direction of spoken language grammar, particularly in recent years (Palmer 1924; Fries 1952; Sinclair 1972a; Brazil 1995; Biber et al 1999 Ch.15; Carter and McCarthy 2006: 82-154). But the bulk of all grammars is focused on the written variety, the spoken form is seen as written language with added problems, and the detailed studies of spoken discourse in the last several decades in the development of Discourse Analysis and Conversation Analysis have not been integrated into the mainstream grammars.

Among the cruder manifestations of this comparative neglect is the use of a largely pejorative terminology. Terminology is supposed to be above earthly things such as connotation or semantic prosody, and linguists may not always be aware of the unavoidable slurs that they routinely cast on the categories of spoken language description. Mostly the underlying suggestion is that spoken language is, in terms of structure and expression, the poor relation of writing. A recent paper by Rühlemann (2006) draws attention to this sorry state of affairs.

Written language variety has been extensively studied; the level of conformity among written varieties is far greater than the similarities between any of these and any impromptu speech event. But within the written variety there are many of what might be called "marginal varieties", so specialised that they hardly look like English at all. Financial reports, telegraphese, chess games, heraldic blazons, sports fixtures and results — grammars normally make no provision for these. The new Linear Unit Grammar, however can accommodate these, and it can also cope with literary text, some of which departs notably from conventions.

Linearity

People experience language as a linear phenomenon, that is, arranged along a single dimension. In the case of spoken language, the dimension is time, while in the written language it is space. Despite the fact that what we write on is usually a flat, two-dimensional surface, we use only one of those dimensions, either the horizontal or the vertical, as the line on which the writing is arranged.

Linearity has been accepted as a fundamental feature of language since Saussure and the dawn of descriptive linguistics. Despite the close connection between gesture, body language and articulation, the linear sound wave remains the essential carrier of language. Written texts are also frequently embellished with decoration, illustrations and non-linear graphs, charts, tables, figures, maps etc., which often form close connections with the linear alphanumeric sequence, and with computer graphics and the internet the opportunities to diverge from strict linearity have changed some aspects of the written text; we can expect that writing will increasingly adapt to these new media, as it did to materials like stone and papyrus in the past.

Some artistic exploitation of the linear forms has always been with us, at least since song brought together music and speech. In the history of writing such traditions as the illuminated manuscript are of considerable antiquity, and in some modern art forms such as concrete poetry or graffiti the writing is arranged in two or even three dimensions, which creates extra meaning, but not of a codified kind. Regarding the spoken language, the sound recording expands the potential for nonlinear communications, which have been exploited in art works from time to time using techniques such as multitracking.

Text archives are now of dimensions so large that it would be impossible to check even if their lists of contents were accurate, far less for anyone actually to read through the constituent documents. The art of finding what you need to read is already rivalling in importance the art of reading it after you have found it, but the only ultimate reason for making such archives is the potential of the documents for being read and understood — i.e. to be interpreted as linear text.

Hierarchy

In sharp contrast to the linearity which is still manifest in almost all text, descriptive grammars are completely non-linear; most of them are presented in very complex hierarchies. Linearity is a property of the physical manifestations of language, and is part of the description of what is present in a text. But the prevalent models of grammar highlight what is *not* present — the choices that could have been made but have been rejected. The sets of choices are called *paradigms*, and the "meaning" of a paradigmatic choice is the sum of the other possible choices that have been rejected. In Firth's famous phrase "A nominative in a four-case system would . . . necessarily have a different 'meaning' from a nominative in a two-case or in a fourteen-case system . . ." (Firth 1957: 227). Also there is usually a choice not to have a choice, so to speak: many paradigmatic systems of choice are optional, leading to further hierarchies of choice, and to philosophical problems about whether a choice of zero is or is not a choice, and whether it is a choice of zero within a paradigmatic system, or a choice not to invoke that system.

Linearity does not survive in this abstract realm except in structural statements when the sequencing of elements has to mirror the physical facts of the text. Our policy is to maintain linearity until we recombine elements so as to be closer to the requirements of a general grammar. The recombination is done with the smallest possible disturbance to the linear sequence because for languages like English the sequencing is critical for determining meaning and so it is retained unless it is incompatible with coherence. See chapter 9.

Chunking

The whole edifice that we build in this book rests on a single supposition — that chunking is a natural and unavoidable way of perceiving language text as it is encountered. Our discussion of relevant literature (see Chapter 2) shows that this is a common supposition, normally taken as self-evident; for example Abney (1991) says categorically "when I read a sentence, I read it a chunk at a time". While we can adduce many similar quotes to Abney's, we are not aware of any counter-claims or counter-evidence. Nobody, it seems, challenges the supposition, and nobody claims that there is no such thing as chunking, or that it is a feature of the perception of only some speakers and not others.

In principle we could have devised a psycholinguistic experiment to bolster our claim, but we have not done so. Such a project would not be easy, because it is very difficult to specify precisely the kind of behaviour that would be required to demonstrate the validity of our supposition. We do not demand a high rate of conformity, of "inter-user reliability", in the jargon; indeed we would be very suspicious of any experimental results that indicated regimented responses. Our supposition can be broken into two subsidiaries — first that to a user of a language any text falls into smallish chunks, and second that there is variation in the perception of where each chunk starts and stops. We cannot declare a maximum number of words in a chunk, though not many contain more than four or five words. The precise boundary marking incorporates low-level variations that indicate differences in interpretation, but not enough to threaten collapse of the communication process, which is quite robust. It is one of the strengths of a language that it can tolerate such variation with apparently little degradation of the medium of communication.

The possibility of experimental confirmation is, however, a live issue, and if our general approach and thesis finds approval then the expenditure of time and effort to substantiate our supposition could be justified. In anticipation of the variation that will be encountered, we suggest that the uniformity of decision will be easiest to handle if expressed negatively; rather than expect subjects to place unit boundaries in certain places, we believe that to note where nobody or hardly anybody places a boundary will be a more fruitful approach.

Here is a starting example of a children's rhyme, with no punctuation, but preserving the stanza structure:

This old man he played one
He played knick knack on my thumb
With a knick knack paddywack give a dog a bone
This old man came rolling home

The last line of this verse could be perceived as a single unit,

1. This old man came rolling home

or it could be divided in various ways, e.g.:

2. This old man | came rolling home
3. This old man | came rolling | home

but never, for example:

4. This | old man came rolling home
5. This old | man came rolling | home

Since it is a children's song with a sing-song rhythm, there is another division that is almost plausible, with a division in front of each beat:

6. This old | man came | rolling | home

However, the divisions of example 6 are mechanical, and indicate a reading that does not follow the meaning.

The possible and unlikely divisions illustrated above show how the chunking "follows" the meaning. Other factors are involved, which accounts for the different decisions that individuals may make. One major dividing point is the boundary between subject and predicate, and examples 2 and 3 make this division; example 3 adds a further division within the predicate, marking the boundary between the verbal elements and the adverb *home*. Example 4 picks out only a very minor boundary, between a determiner and the remainder of the noun group, and none elsewhere in the line; this division is unmotivated by any considerations of meaning, rhythm or balance. Example 5 is more balanced, but the divisions are in minor places, cutting off the head noun *man* from its modifiers and the verb from its adverb, while the major possible boundaries are ignored; this is another unmotivated division.

Analysis

The central question in linguistics is *how do speakers make meaning by making text*? To shape an answer to this question, Linear Unit Grammar begins by pursuing the hypothesis, discussed above, that there is sufficient similarity of interpretive strategies among individual users of English for them to guide us towards finding chunk boundaries. Having determined provisional boundaries, the chunks so formed are classified using a well-known technique of descriptive grammar: a small set of descriptive categories is proposed, with clear working definitions for each, and with rules for their occurrence and combination. The set of categories is used to describe a portfolio of samples of English in action, and the descriptions are presented in the following pages. The scope, accuracy and value of the analysis are discussed.

The categories are arranged in *delicacy*—that is, we identify sub-types of the original distinctions. The distinctions are essentially *systemic* in Halliday's sense (1961), in that they are small sets of mutually exclusive choices that come into play under designated conditions. We have only proposed the minimal number of categories that we require to account for our data, and we are following the strategy of setting up the simplest possible apparatus that will allow an adequate description to emerge. But the system of analysis has the potential of modest extension for encountering structural patterns which are not exemplified in the sample material.

This flexibility within a simple apparatus, plus its ability to cope with the wide range of texts encountered in the samples, allows us to claim that the descriptive system is robust.

One grammar

At the beginning of this chapter we contrasted the reality of the many varieties of a language with the generally-held view that a single grammar can make an adequate description of them all. It is necessary to be clear about what we mean by "a single grammar". Its singularity is in relation to the many varieties of register, genre etc. into which language text is normally divided; in particular we are concerned with the differences — substantial on the surface — between spoken and written modes. At present the principal technique for yoking both together is to see spoken text as a degenerate version of writing, and this book is, we hope, a strong testament against that position. But if the observed features of spoken text are given genuinely equal status vis-à-vis written text, then the kind of analysis and resulting description that we offer here will, we claim, be found necessary.

It is to be noted that in a rather crude but familiar classification of grammars, Linear Unit Grammar is a "bottom-up" grammar; it begins by examination of textual data and takes progressive steps in generalisation and abstraction, each one aimed at relating different manifestations of language to each other. There is no end point specified. "Top-down" grammars, whether or not they pay close attention to data, begin with a highly abstract representation of a sentence (e.g. "S") and anatomise it step by step in an effort to coincide with actual text.

There are two points to be made about this contrast. In the first case, a genuine bottom-up grammar would attract no following at all because it would not engage with meaning. The only way we have at present to engage with meaning is to use intuition, and intuition is definitely at the top, having the qualities more of the Delphic oracle than of a scientific investigation. Its chief quality is to evaluate difference of meaning; since any two pieces of text that differ in form must, prima facie, differ in meaning, the intuition is able to judge whether a difference is minor or major. If minor, the two pieces of text can be linked as paraphrases of each other; if major they can not. This facility for intuitive judgment works in the same way for any competent language user. So "bottom-up" refers only to the direction of the analysis, and not to the analytic tools.

The second point is that "top-down" grammars which perform an analysis in a single pass through the grammar will come under ever-increasing pressure from corpus-aware users that their statements do not tally with the observations. Where the form of the grammar is a totally coherent formal algorithm, this is already well understood, but the less formal grammars have retained some leeway. However, recent research suggests more and more strongly that any such description would be at odds with the meaning made by texts; indeed any description that proceeds rigorously top down from a single starting point and hopes to culminate in a precise description of the meaning of actual texts, is doomed to failure.

The system described in these pages offers only the first few steps towards an adequate grammar — but these are essential steps and largely overlooked. The input is almost any text written or spoken in English, and the output is (a) a text which is close to an acceptable input to a conventional grammar, accompanied by (b) informal notes on aspects of the interaction which are not recorded in the output text.

Word-by-word description

Before presenting a systematic description of the grammar, let us go through a sample text transcript in an informal manner, word by word, noting our perceptions of structure and meaning, and, as far as possible, reasons for them. The remainder of this chapter sets out speculatively the kind of analytical judgments that we believe people have access to.

Example 1.
The following is a fragment from a recorded conversation,[1] transcribed without punctuation or capital letters.

> i havent i didnt see anything because it was during the night but it we we crossed to denmark in the morning

How does a competent user of English make sense out of this? The first move in interpretation is so swift and natural that it is not often noticed; for this reason we have featured it in the Preamble; the reader intuitively gives boundary status to the wider gaps between characters, and the word forms are thus already on the table. The same text without this aid to interpretation is:

> ihaventididntseeanythingbecauseitwasduringthe
> nightbutitwewecrossedtodenmarkinthemorning

Let us give a consecutive number to each of the word forms since several are repeated.

1. i	2. havent	3. i	4. didnt	5. see	6. anything
7. because	8. it	9. was	10. during	11. the	12. night

---

[1] This extract comes from the Lexis text, which was the first fragment that was analysed for the study. The last few words are the first few words of the passage chosen for full step-by-step description later in this book.

13. but	14. it	15. we	16. we	17. crossed	18. to
19. denmark	20. in	21. the	22. morning		

The aim of this study is to divide the text up into small stretches of a few words each, using general perceptions concerning the nature of text, which we share.

Words 1–8
Let us consider the first pair of words, W1 and W2, and then add the rest one at a time in text sequence. It is not suggested that readers in normal circumstances use such tactics, but it allows a careful discussion of the effect of each word and the cumulative experience of the text.

W1 and W2 together suggest a familiar structure, which will not be named at present because we do not want to invoke the assumptions of established grammar. It is, however, probably incomplete because we normally expect something else after W2 (see the discussion of completeness in Chapter 11). Since the sample passage begins here, we have no record of what preceded W1, and this is what is causing the uncertainty; W2 could only be completive if it followed an utterance which contained *have* and a suitable completion — like a question "Have you read this book?", where *i havent* would be part of an acceptable response.

As it happens, we do have access to the transcript immediately before the quoted passage; the previous few word forms are:

i havent seen it went through germany but of course

There is nothing here that would allow *i havent* to be completive, but we note that the first two words of this previous fragment are the same as W1 and W2, so W1 and W2 can be interpreted as some kind of return to them, a re-start. The completion of *i havent* in this fragment is *seen it*, but the intervening material (*went through germany but of course*) obliges us to regard W1 and W2 as a new construction, not dependent on preceding material.

There is thus an expectation that a completion of the W1 W2 pair will have to follow W2, so we look at the next word. W3 is the same as W1 and it cannot complete the pair because it is a unique form in English and it cannot be a completive in a declarative clause. Again we do not really need to invoke the apparatus of conventional grammar, but merely establish that W1 W2 is not completed by W3, and W3 is now the focus of an emerging pattern.

Our first interpretation of this situation is that W3 begins a new structure and therefore W1 and W2 comprise an incomplete structure. It is not the only interpretation — we may be in the middle of a "garden path" structure whose logic will be revealed later (see, for example, http://www.fun-with-words.com/ambiguous_garden_path.html). But unless later events contradict our first interpretation we will stick to that, and bring in W4.

W4, *didnt,* is similar in function to W2 and we can make the same provisional categorisation of W3 W4 as incomplete. Because of the similarity of the pairs W1 W2 and W3 W4 we can also explain the incompleteness of W1 W2 as follows: the speaker wanted to return to the matter of what could or could not be seen, and returned to an earlier phrasing, but almost immediately thought better of it and altered the succeeding phraseological options by replacing W2 by W4, *havent* by *didnt*.

On the basis of this argument we can separate W1 and W2 from what follows by declaring a chunk, chunk A, and assigning W1 and W2 to it. The white space between W2 and W3 is now designated a Provisional Unit Boundary (PUB) and we make a fresh start with W3 and W4.

We now add W5, *see*. W5 is understandable as a continuation of the structure created by W3 and W4, but is still not complete. Also, going back to the recall of the conversation prior to W1, the repetition of the verb *seen* as *see* confirms the hypothesis that W1–W5 recall *i havent seen…* from the text that immediately precedes our extract.

W6 is *anything*, and offers a completion to the evolving structure. We assume that the speaker has been asked if he had seen something, and answered first that he had not (W1 W2), and then, by way of explanation, that he did not see anything at all, rather than that he missed whatever he was asked about. The segment W3–W6 is a possible chunk, so we approach W7 with the expectation that it may well start a new structure.

W7 is *because*, and we recognise it as a word whose function is to start something new. So we can confidently declare chunk B as W3–W6, assign a chunk boundary between W6 and W7, and we have a consistent and plausible interpretation of the passage up to this point.

chunk	numbers	words
A	1,2	i havent
B	3,4,5,6	*i didn't see anything*

W7 is almost certainly in a chunk by itself. We do not have a record of how closely it was related in pronunciation to the words on either side, but it certainly performs a different function from them; it links chunk B with the following chunk which begins with W8.

In conventional grammar W7 would be considered the first word in a clause which provides a reason for chunk B; hence it is likely that someone who had even a passing acquaintance with English grammar would not be inclined to assign *because* to its own chunk. But this disinclination is probably more learned than intuitive, and we will elaborate the point before returning to our specimen text.

Clause boundaries
This is, then, a brief excursion into conventional grammar. Given the sentence:

> I didn't see anything because it was during the night.

an uncontroversial analysis would be:

main clause:	I didn't see anything
subordinate clause:	because it was during the night.

That is to say, there is a convention in the grammar that a subordinate clause includes the marker of subordination, leaving the main clause without any indication that there is any other clause dependent on it. A strong case could be made for an alternative division:

main clause:	I didn't see anything because
subordinate clause:	it was during the night.

It is important to note that this is little more than a notational variant of the normal version — there is no suggestion that it is a different analysis in the sense that there are different relations among the elements. It is just that the mark of subordination is placed in the other clause, and for some purposes this can be a convenient representation. In the conventional analysis, the first one, the main clause looks exactly the same as a simple sentence containing the same words, and this can lead to mild confusion. In this version it is the subordinate clause that looks like a simple sentence, but we know that neither of them has the status and all the properties of a simple sentence because the two clauses are interdependent.

A third notational variant expresses clearly the interdependence of the clauses:

main clause:	I didn't see anything because
subordinate clause:	because it was during the night.

The conjunction *because* is expressed in both clauses, emphasising that neither of them is complete in itself. While this is an elegant solution, maintaining the normal conventions of the grammar, it is dubious from a theoretical point of view, because the device of including the same element of structure in two clauses runs contrary to any normal appreciation of the segmentation of an utterance.

There is a fourth possibility, which seems to express the relationships without resort to devices:

main clause:	I didn't see anything
relational element:	because
subordinate clause:	it was during the night

The argument of this notation is that the word *because* belongs to neither clause, but expresses the relationship between the two clauses, and is neither a clause nor a part of a clause. It is called a *relational element* here to emphasise that this is a fairly radical departure from conventional grammar.

This is a sensible, simple and clear analysis of the original sentence. The reason why it is not a popular expression of the structure is probably because most grammars feature the kind of organisation set out in Halliday's "taxonomic hierarchy" (op.cit.), so that a sentence must be made up of one or more clauses and nothing else; nothing that is not a clause is permitted to appear. This suggests that the proposal to divide the sentence into three units moves the discussion from notation to theory.

In this book we try to maintain a linear boundary assignment, and so the last representation of the structure is the closest to our needs. We would propose a first, shallow analysis of the passage as:

chunk B: I didnt see anything
chunk C: because
chunk D: it was during the night

This allows us to recombine the elements in several different ways in a later, less shallow analysis. It is perfectly compatible with a conventional analysis which would simply merge C and D.

Words 8–13
Returning to the interpretation of the transcript, this argument gives us W7 as chunk C, and W8 as starting a new chunk. In passing we note that we now have three different kinds of chunk: chunk A is an incomplete structure, chunk B is a complete one, and chunk C mediates between structures rather than realises one in itself.

We can now add W9, *was*. This combines with W8 in a familiar structure, similar to W1W2 and W3W4, and it is also incomplete so far because the word *was* indicates a need for something to follow. We add in W10, so that we are holding three words in the processing area. W10, *during,* is the possible start of a completion, but it requires completion itself, so the unfolding structure remains open and we continue by adding W11, *the*. This word is also a reasonable continuation of the pattern W8–W10, but once again it does not complete a pattern, so we add in a fifth word, W12. There are now four words prospecting completion — *it, was, during* and *the*. W12 is *night*, and happily completes all four of the prospections. First it combines with W11 as *the night*, then these two combine with W10 as *during the night*, and these three combine with W9 to make *was during the night*; finally the whole sequence completes the prospection of W8, *it*.

Five words is close to the maximum number that regularly fits into a chunk. In this case there is no satisfactory word-break between 9 and 12 where a boundary could be reasonably inserted, because each of W9–11 adds its own incompleteness. This type of analysis has been developed in literary stylistics (Sinclair 1972; forthcoming 2007), calling attention to a kind of syntactical energy that builds up towards a multiple completion. We are thus poised to place a chunk boundary after W12. W13 is *but*, and confirms the need for a boundary, so W8–W12 are assigned to chunk D.

chunk	numbers	words
A	1,2	i havent
B	3,4,5,6	i didnt see anything
C	7	because
D	8,9,10,11,12	*it was during the night*

For W13 we invoke the same argument as for W7. W14 is *it*, and this combination would make an acceptable clause opening; however, as we have recently argued, the word *but* relates the preceding chunk or chunks to those which succeed it, and it plays no internal part in the structure of either. We shall see in a moment a practical reason to go with the theoretical point that *but* should be a chunk on its own; just as W7, *because*, became chunk C, then W13 becomes chunk E.

Words 14–15
We postulate a new chunk beginning with W14, *it*, and go on to consider W15, *we*. There is no obvious structure that begins *it we*, and so we provisionally assign W14 to an incomplete chunk F; we do this provisionally because there is a tiny chance that W14 and W15 begin a marginal structure like ?"It we expect to be expensive, but what about the other?". While technically possible, there are no instances of this

structure in The Bank of English at 520 million words, so we can safely forget it.

We now turn to W16, which is a second *we*. This is a common event in unscripted speech, where the speaker changes tack and begins again. In a case like this one the restart is the same as the one abandoned. The real-time record shows that the speaker decides not to pursue another structure starting with *it* and switches to *we*; is not fully committed to that opening immediately, but confirms it by repeating the word in W16.

Such revisions of tactics are very common in informal spoken language, and are largely missing from written documents; missing because they are suppressed, not because the writer did not go through similar experiences. They usually get names like "false start", "hesitation", which suggest that they are blemishes on the speaker's performance, although they are closer to indications of tactical skill.

In our simple linear chunking analysis we assign W15 to another chunk G, noting that like its predecessor it is incomplete. The speaker announces a change of direction with *but* and searches for a suitable opening, which turns out to be *we*, and the new structure opens with W16 and continues with W17, *crossed*, with which it forms a recognised structural pattern.

chunk	numbers	words	notes
A	1,2	i havent	incomplete
B	3,4,5,6	i didnt see anything	
C	7	because	relational
D	8,9,10,11,12	it was during the night	
E	13	but	relational
F	14	it	incomplete
G	15	we	incomplete

Words 16–22
W16 and W17 make up a potentially complete structure because *crossed* does not always require a continuation; these two words make up a viable chunk, but a small one, and *crossed* is very often followed by an object or a locational expression. So we look ahead a bit, leaving the opportunity to return to a chunk boundary after W17. W18 is *to* and we appreciate that this word could initiate an optional continuation, but requires completion, so we continue, leaving the structure open. W19 is *denmark*, which is a suitable completion, so the structure is again able to stand on its own; we can opt for a four-word chunk W16–W19. However we are not yet at the limits of chunk size, so we can have a look at W20, which is *in*. Like W18, *to*, this probably opens another optional continuation, and so we go on to W21 *the*, and W22, *morning*. The situation is similar to chunk D in that W22 fulfils the prospections of W21 and W20.

There are now seven words in the processing area, and this is unusually long for a chunk, though there is no specific upper boundary. Also we have noted two places along the way where it would be quite acceptable to divide the segment.

The options are:

1. one single chunk *we crossed to denmark in the morning*
2. two chunks (ai) *we crossed to denmark* (aii) *in the morning*
    (bi) *we crossed* (bii) *to denmark in the morning*
3. three chunks (i) *we crossed* (ii) *to denmark* (iii) *in the morning*

Of these, option 2b is the least likely, perhaps because *to denmark* and *in the morning* are separately associated with *we crossed*, and are not specially related to each other (if the transcript had read "we crossed from Germany to Denmark", a division like 2b would be justified). Among the other options, we can only report personal experience. The authors, analysing separately, agreed on the first comparison of their decisions on option 2a. It seems that *crossed*, while not requiring a continuation, does seem to attract it, and so there is no strong motivation for a chunk boundary after *crossed*; we therefore reject option 3. However, the lack of structural cohesion between *to denmark* and *in the morning*, combined with the growing size of the chunk at four words, tips the balance in favour of a boundary after W19.

In a conventional grammar, this whole segment would make up a single clause, and it is clear that the last phrase is structurally dependent on the preceding chunk, though not on the immediately preceding words. As a chunk, it is a new variety, a continuation of an established pattern. But if we ignored the step of chunking we would miss one point — that option 2b is not felt to be a natural grouping.

The result of this exercise is:

chunk	numbers	words	notes
A	1,2	i havent	incomplete
B	3,4,5,6	i didnt see anything	complete
C	7	because	relational
D	8,9,10,11,12	it was during the night	complete
E	13	but	relational
F	14	it	incomplete
G	15	we	incomplete
H:	16,17,18,19	we crossed to denmark	complete
I:	20,21,22	in the morning	continuation

There are four kinds of chunk so far. We believe that other competent users of English would make a similar assignment of boundaries, and that any differences in assignment would be capable of reconciliation at a later stage. The only case where there were genuine options came at the end, and we chose the middle course of three reasonable possibilities. As a precautionary measure while this kind of analysis is still novel, we recommend the placement of a boundary in cases of doubt, because it is easier to delete it at a later stage than to find it again within a chunk. So if *to denmark* is assigned to a separate chunk (option 3), then that is perhaps even safer than the analysis that we offer above, although we feel it is less natural.

We do not support any additional or alternative chunk boundaries in this passage; if *during the night*, for example was proposed as a separate chunk we would argue that this makes *it was* into an incomplete structure, which cannot be followed by a continuation. It is clear that some sort of syntax begins to grow naturally from these arguments.

We have made a case for a non-hierarchical treatment of words and phrases that express relationships, like *because* and *but* in the passage above. We argue that the motivation for attaching these words to the structures that follow them is merely a convention, and flows from an absolute requirement of some theories that a sentence must be made up of one or more than one complete clauses, and nothing else. While such a model may well be found suitable ultimately, at this very first stage of analysis we see no reason to apply such a stricture, and in the chunking so far we can already see a good reason. If W13 *but* had been attached to W14 *it*, then it would have had to be detached again when *it* turned out to be incomplete. It would then be attached to W15 *we*, but since this is also an incomplete structure, *but* would have had to stretch over two words in order to be attached to W16 *we*, so that it could begin a completed structure.

There are two reasons to reject the argument that our texts must all be divided into clauses. One is that it is not necessary, as we have already shown. The other is that it is very likely to be inaccurate, since when the speaker uttered *but* it was something of a place-holder and general indicator of a change of direction, and not a conjunction opening a clause that was already thought out in its entirety, as would be expected of it in conventional grammar.

Example 2 — with turntaking
The extract discussed above shows something of the organisation of conversation, which we have marked by assigning provisional boundaries that divide the continuous text into chunks; in passing we have noted that there are several kinds of chunk. In order to broaden the range of structures and types, we will now go through another extract from the same conversation,[2] but at a faster pace. In view

---

2. This extract comes from later in the transcription, after the passage chosen for step-by-step analysis.

of the explicitness of the previous section, we will cut a few corners and miss out a few caveats.

> from hamburg to copenhagen you know you have to go
> by several islands oh no the train went on the boat did it

We number the words again for reference:

1. from	2. hamburg	3. to	4. copenhagen	5. you
6. know	7. you	8. have	9. to	10. go
11. by	12. several	13. islands	14. oh	15. no
16. the	17. train	18. went	19. the	20. train
21. went	22. on	23. the	24. boat	25. did
26. it				

Words 1–6
W1W2 make up a familiar structure, but not a self-standing unit, so they either open a continuation of a previous unit or prospect one to follow closely. The previous few words are:

> does the train go on the boat going from yes

There is no indication of speaker change in this transcript, but it must be invoked here as the likeliest explanation of *from yes*. If these two words are said by different participants then the second speaker takes over the initiative but co-operatively continues the topic, indicating this by repeating *from* as W1.

W3, *to*, could indicate a boundary, but there is a connection between *from…* and *to…* that suggests they might stay together. W4, *copenhagen*, like W2, *hamburg*, is recognisable as a place name, so the four words go well together. There is no complete structural pattern as yet, however, though this segment could be interpreted as a continuation of the previous speaker's structure, and a boundary could be inserted after W4. But let us see what comes next — W5, W6 is *you know*, and this phrase is one of the commonest interactive gestures, which we can confidently make into a separate chunk because of this function.

With this argument we can declare chunk A as W1–W4, and chunk B as W5 W6. The next word is W7, *you* again and W8 is *have*. This begins to look like the kind of structure that we have been waiting for, and W9, *to*, and W10, *go* are sufficient to clinch the issue. We assign W5 W6 to chunk B, noting that this is a different kind of chunk than any we have had before — a little like *because* and *but*, but independent of the surrounding structures, a valid structure in its own right, and contributing to the management of the interaction. The difference to bear in mind is that between, for example, "You know that he's angry." and "He's angry, you know." In the first (invented) example what the speaker avers is known is the clause that follows, while in the second it is quite likely that his being angry is news to the listener, and the phrase "you know" is of a slightly sinister nature, suggesting unfortunate consequences of his being angry. In the second pattern the phrase serves to present "He's angry" in a suitable context, rather than having anything to do with knowledge.

We now see that chunk A is a transitional segment, capable of being interpreted either as a completion of the previous speaker's utterance, or as an early-placed adverbial related to *go*, W10. Or it could remain transitional, as spoken structures can, and do double duty. We return to this question later on.

Words 7–26
We now build up the next chunk. W7–W10 do not attract a boundary because *have to* is interpreted as a single unit, a modal verb like *must*. While these words form a possible chunk, it is not complete because the verb *go* usually requires something to indicate direction, speed or the like. The situation is similar to W17 *crossed* in the first extract. W11 is *by*, starting a suitable continuation of W7–W10, so we leave the structure open and add W12, *several* and W13, *islands*. Here there is a very suitable place for a chunk boundary, and after seven words it would be a lengthy one. It is likely that some people would prefer a boundary after W10, but it is not necessary, and for this analysis the decision is to recognise chunk C as the whole of W7–W13.

W14 is *oh* and W15 is *no*, which suggests a very common interjection, probably a speaker change, confirming the end of chunk C. W16, *the* appears to start another chunk, so provisionally we assign W14 W15 to chunk D. W17 *train* confirms a return to the main topic. W18 *went* makes a recognised structure with W17 but, as before in W10, there is need for a completion of the structure following *went*. W19, *the* is an unlikely starting point for a completion, but it is not impossible, so we suspend judgment and consider W20, *train*. Suspicions are aroused because *the train went the train* is incoherent, and W21, *went*, confirms that W16–W18 make up an incomplete chunk, which is repeated exactly in W19–W21. This is chunk E.

W19–W21 is still not complete, so we consider W22, *on*, and find it a reasonable start for the continuation that is prospected, and W23, W24, *the boat*, provide a reasonable completion. W25, *did* is clearly off somewhere else, so we can assign W19–W24 to chunk F, with a boundary following W24. W26 is *it*, and we note that *did it* is a suitable tag to chunk F; since we are now at the end of the extract we can assign WW25, 26 to chunk G and might indicate a speaker change as well after W24.

The analysis now looks like:

chunk	numbers	words	notes
A	1,2,3,4	from hamburg to copenhagen	transitional
B	5,6	you know	relational
C	7,8,9,10,11,12,13	you have to go by several islands	complete
D	14,15	oh no	relational
E	16,17,18	the train went	incomplete
F	19,20,21,22,23,24	the train went on the boat	complete
G	25,26	did it	relational

It is helpful at this point to review the speaker changes. If speaker α utters chunks A, B and C, and speaker β utters chunk D, then does the first speaker take over again immediately? Since speaker α is responsible for the narrative, and is the person who knows about this journey, it seems likely that he utters chunks E and F, while speaker β (or indeed speaker γ, δ or ε) utters chunk G.

The result of this analysis is as follows:

chunk	speaker	words	notes
A	α	from hamburg to copenhagen	transitional
B	α	you know	relational
C	α	you have to go by several islands	complete
D	β	oh no	relational
E	α	the train went	incomplete
F	α	the train went on the boat	complete
G	β	did it	relational

We can now review the different kinds of chunk that we have noted. There are two "complete" chunks which contain most of the narrative, and an incomplete one, chunk E. There are three relational chunks but these are much more concerned with the interaction than those of the first passage, and indeed chunks D and G are almost certainly complete turns. The first chunk we have called "transitional" because it can be interpreted as a continuation of the preceding material but it also has the effect of framing the statements to follow. We cannot recapture the intonation, which might have told us more, but it turns out not to be important.

It is fairly easy, after this very simple analysis, to retrieve the "story-line" of this passage. The speakers co-operated to construct something like the following:

From hamburg to copenhagen you have to go by several islands; the train went on the boat.

The first unit and the two complete ones are just concatentated. The incomplete unit and the relational ones are left out. For comparison, the narrative of the first extract, using only the complete units, is:

I didnt see anything, it was during the night, we crossed to denmark in the morning.

Here the coherence is improved by adding in the relational elements:

I didnt see anything because it was during the night, but we crossed to denmark in the morning.

Conclusion

The second extract included some likely speaker changes, but apart from those we did not find a lot of new material, and the inventory of different kinds of PUBs and chunks was not greatly enlarged.

Because we do not have recourse to a more detailed transcript nor to the original sound recording, these extracts bring out the co-operative side of conversation rather than the more competitive side that comes out in discourse analysis. Features of the delivery, of contextual conditions, even of who said what, are not given the same prominence that they have in the familiar descriptions of verbal intereaction; this analysis highlights the achievement of a coherent sharing of verbal experience.

In this chapter we have raised most of the concepts that are needed for the analysis, and gone through some examples in a particularly thorough fashion, so that the task of the next section is largely a matter of systematisation of the analysis, settling on suitable terms and applying the analysis to a number of widely differing texts to show its adaptability.

CHAPTER 2

Background

Many theoretical models and empirical studies have a bearing on the ideas and the system of analysis that this book offers. This chapter discusses some of the earlier work that has been done in areas which are most relevant to the present work. Some of these have had a profound influence on our thinking, others appear to be ploughing the same field but on closer inspection turn out to be quite distant. We have made a narrow rather than broad selection in the interests of keeping the discussion brief, but we look into models of grammar which have tackled the question of linearity in one way or another, and previous approaches to dealing with chunks of online speech whether these take syntax, intonation, cognitive processing or language learning as their point of departure

The ideas that are developed in this book are not new; the novelty is in the selection and blending of them into a coherent theoretical stance and a practical analytical system. The matter of chunking crops up from time to time in different areas of linguistic work, and seems to be a robust and primitive notion; if so it is important to keep its pre-theoretical status. Attempts to maintain the linearity of text in description, and to accept the theoretical consequences of this, are not uncommon and keep re-appearing despite being condemned in advance to failure by influential voices in current linguistics. And yet we find that theorists, some of whom are instanced below and who work at the formal end of the linguistic spectrum argue cases that harmonise with our data-immersed hypotheses.

Immediate constituent analysis

We begin with the influential descriptions of English of about half a century ago in USA, called *immediate constituent analysis*. As the word "immediate" suggests, these are grammars of surface structure. While there are many versions of IC grammar, for students, teachers and researchers, perhaps the finest is that of Eugene Nida, *A synopsis of English Syntax* (Nida 1960). It is brief but packed, an edited version of Nida's Ph.D. thesis done for the University of Michigan in 1943. Its publication some seventeen years after completion seems to have been stimulated by the emergence of transformational grammar in the late fifties; its preface (ibid: iv, v) lists grammars by Harris, Wells, Fries and influential publications by Chomsky, Pike and Bar-Hillel, bearing witness to the formidable range of descriptive activity that was going on in USA at that time. However, IC analysis was the most popular and typical model of the period up to the early nineteen-sixties.

While conceding something like deep structure in a newly-written Preface, Nida nevertheless presents his Synopsis defiantly and claims that it is published in response to demand, not only as being the most extensive treatment of the descriptive system but also as containing "many useful lists of words functioning as syntactic classes" (1960:vi). Given that even large modern grammars are often sparing with lists of class members, this latter feature of the book ensured its enduring reputation as a seminal work.

Nida's grammar places one of four relationships at word boundaries, though because of a hierarchy that is erected in the analysis, the boundary is often of a unit larger than a word. *Exocentric* is the kind of relationship that is made by subject and predicate, or between a preposition and the following noun phrase; the items related have quite different syntactic roles, and extend the expressive possibilities of the language. *Endocentric* relations are the opposite — the items involved collaborate in the construction of a single linguistic entity like a noun phrase; there are two kinds, *co-ordinate* and *subordinate*. Finally, a juxtaposition of items, as in apposition or after sentence adverbs like *nevertheless*, is called *paratactic*.

So in a sentence like the one below, the relations are progressively marked as the hierarchy is built up:

Sorry,	the	boys	heard	you	and	ran	away
	↑ sub. endocentric		↑ sub. endocentric			↑ sub. endocentric	
	↑ exocentric				↑ exocentric		
	↑ co-ordinate endocentric						
↑ paratactic						

Each word space carries one of four boundaries, so in that sense it has a linear representation, but the boundaries have implications of a hierarchy; in a regular clause like *the boys heard you*, the endocentric structures are found within the exocentric one; the *and* joins two clauses and so the two exocentric clauses are placed within it; the *sorry* is seen as external to the rest of the sentence, making a paratactic structure which is the outermost layer.

This layering depends to some extent on the details of the structure, so that an *and* in between two subject nouns, as in *Bill and Tom left* joins *Bill* and *Tom* in a co-ordinate endocentric structure within the exocentric structure of the subject and predicate of the clause. So there is an implicit recognition of a scale of units. Discontinuous structures like *Did the man leave?* are handled with less elegance, because the first boundary, between *Did* and *the*, has no structural value, nor has the last boundary, *man/leave*, since the grammatical interpretation is that the two major components, making the outermost level, are *the man* and *Did…leave*. A clumsy convention of crossing lines is necessary to accommodate this clear departure from linearity, and it is on evidence of this kind that Chomsky based his rejection of structure being representable by a Markovian model (1957: 21–4).

From the many books and papers which describe IC analysis we have picked out Nida because it is a thorough academic work and because we adopt some of his terminology later in this book, with alterations. A more familiar version of IC analysis can be found in, for example, Francis (1963), where there are fifty or so pages of accessible description. Francis would analyse the example sentence as follows:

Sorry,	the	boys	heard	you	and	ran	away
	↑ modification		↑ complementation			↑ modification	
		↑ predication					
					↑ co-ordination		
↑ sentence modifier							

In Francis's system of analysis, a co-ordinator like *and* contracts the same relationship on both sides.

When the surge of generative-transformational grammar (TG) starting around 1963 swept all this away, it did not replace it with an alternative procedure that was comprehensive and robust enough to be used in all the practical applications, especially those that require simple analysis of a non-technical nature. The focus of attention was "deep" structure, and the kind of analysis portrayed above was dubbed "surface structure" and held to be of little interest.

To begin with, it was imagined that the new grammar would be fully explicit and therefore compatible with the rigours of computational representation, which was becoming fashionable in the analysis of language, and indeed the formalism of TG was influential in the early days of computational linguistics. However, it gradually became clear that the complexity of a fully explicit grammar was beyond the abilities of that generation of scholars and machines, and also of those that have succeeded them.

After some years attention returned to the practical matter of finding a means of describing a wide range of sentences, without too much attention being paid to the deep structure. With that change of emphasis, and with a growing interest in deriving information from large corpora, notions like *partial parsing, shallow parsing* and *local grammars* emerged. Instead of trying to derive each sentence from a primitive logical structure through a maze of rules that impinge on each other, one could concentrate on the text itself and look at the rules that shape it. With partial parsing the scholar chooses an area of interest like multi-word technical terms and works out a detailed grammar for these only (Yang 1986; Coniam 1998; Hasegawa et al 2004). The rest of the grammar was just ignored. Local grammars are similar but arise from a different perception — that no matter how carefully compiled a grammar could be, ordinary open text would continually produce stretches of language that could not be described in a big general grammar. Specialised grammars are necessary for such jobs, originally conceived as minor matters (Gross 1993) but growing in importance and seen as applicable to highly specialised varieties (Barnbrook and Sinclair 2001).

Partial parsing

In one popular variety of shallow parsing, the notion of chunking is the starting point. The leading figure here is Abney, whose much-quoted paper (1991) starts as follows:

> I begin with an intuition: when I read a sentence, I read it a chunk at a time. For example, the previous sentence breaks up something like this:
>
> (1) [I begin] [with an intuition]: [when I read] [a sentence], [I read it] [a chunk] [at a time]

Abney claims that there is evidence for chunks from both prosody (strong stresses) and grammar (content words), and sets out to show both that computer parse strategies are helped by chunking, and also that humans might use a similar method.

Abney is not the originator of the notion of chunking in this usage; he credits another often-quoted paper in cognitive psychology with the main argument. This is Gee and Grosjean (1983), who in turn rely on phonological theories such as Selkirk (1984) and propose to describe read-out sentences in terms of a hierarchy of phonological units, of which an intermediate one called a φ-phrase is the centre of attention. A φ-phrase ends with a word which is the head of a syntactic phrase, and lies hierarchically between a stress-group (which contains one stressed syllable) and an I-phrase, which contains one intonation contour. The φ-phrase is thus a critical link between the phonology and the syntax; the input to the analytical procedure is a parsed sentence and its output is a prediction of the stresses and pauses that readers will make at different reading speeds. The chunks of Abney's initial sentence (above) are φ-phrases.

Abney recognises that "there are two sources of non-determinism in the chunker" (1991:8). One is that the placing of boundaries is variable, and the other, familiar to all parsers of English, is that many word forms could be either nouns or verbs. However, chunking facilitates the separation of heuristic information from grammatical, which Abney believes will improve the performance of a parser. This leads him to a strategic model which starts off in an indeterminate state and strives to reduce the indeterminism as it goes along; it thus often opens more than one alternative analysis, both of the structural value of an item and also of the likelihood of a φ-phrase boundary, and then attempts to close off all but one alternative.

Abney stresses the value of modularity in his model; chunking allows a two-stage process to be devised, with the resolution of uncertainties within the chunk being done separately from what he calls *attachment*, the resolution of uncertainties between one chunk and another. For example he says that "lexical ambiguity is often resolvable within chunks" (1991:5). So even if the chunks are somewhat arbitrary and the boundaries uncertain, they serve a strategic purpose in that the tasks can be broken down into simple routines, with better chances of accuracy and resolution and a better environment for debugging the programs.

This shape of model is potentially attractive to us because, in the chunking and the progressive reduction of uncertainty it has features in common with the natural strategies of people conversing or reading. The major difference is that Abney takes for granted the existence of suitable formal grammars (although "toy" ones at the time he was writing), whereas we are facing a less regulated situation. Also, we are not on this occasion aiming at the design of a formal grammar or parser, because we are expanding the range of material that is normally described. But nevertheless it is encouraging to note (a) that the procedures we posit for a language user coping with text in a natural situation are not unlike those that have been found convenient for the precise description of selected, well-formed sentences, and (b) that algorithms and procedures already exist which could be suitable for our material should we continue towards formalism.

Grammar of speech

Perhaps the closest work to ours is that of Brazil (1995), whose *Grammar of Speech* sets out to be "a linear, real-time description of syntax" (ibid:14). Brazil's particular expertise was in intonation, and the book deals exclusively with the spoken language; the impetus to work on grammar arose from his wish to integrate phonological patterns, particularly suprasegmental ones like those of stress and intonation, into the grammar. So he does not start with sentences, and he does not assume that a communicative act exists before it is interpreted — instead it unfolds in time.

Brazil begins with the assumption that speakers "are engaged in the pursuit of some communicative purpose" (ibid: 39), and proceed by *increments* towards the achievement of that purpose. His book is mostly about "telling increments" by which a story is told. Participants recognise three states of the discourse — an initial state, where the participants accept their roles and responsibilities, a target state, where the incrementation has been succesfully achieved, and in between these an intermediate state, where there is an obligation on the speaker to continue until the target state is achieved. In a conventional subject /predicate increment like *She'd been shopping* (ibid: 47), the target state is the completion of the increment and the intermediate state is after *She*, where the speaker is committed to continue.

As Brazil is quick to point out, this is rather a heavy-handed way to describe a non-controversial structure, but he contends that he is setting up a different conceptual framework that leads to substantial differences in the account of how meaning is created by talking. And indeed, it is an inspirational approach which has influenced our work substantially. We adopt Brazil's general stance, that utterances make meaning as they unfold, not after they are finished; we adopt his term *increment* for one of our major categories of structure, and we agree with him in putting as first priority in theory the assumption that users of a language use it in order to communicate.

We do not, however, confine ourselves to the spoken language and, since we are working without access to sound recordings or phonetic transcriptions we do not make assumptions about stress and intonation — merely a few speculations in marginal cases. Brazil indicated (1995: 11–12) that he thought writing would be none the worse for exposure to a real-time grammar, but used Halliday's distinction ("writing exists whereas speech happens" — 1985:xxiii) to postpone that particular issue. We are happy to take up the cudgels here and pursue Brazil's basic model into the arena of ordinary written documents. Halliday's gnomic distinction can be countered by demonstrating two things. In the first place, sound recording allows speech to exist as permanently as writing; however it is important to concede that this technology, after fifty years or so, seems to have had little effect on the structure of spontaneous speech. Secondly, and more to the point, writing, to the reader, unfolds in time. Even when the written language is carved in stone, a reader reads it incrementally, and the existence of what has not been read is as irrelevant to what is being read as if it had not yet occurred.

In the later chapters of *A Grammar of Speech*, Brazil considers aspects of spoken text other than sequences of telling increments. He notes various kinds of organising moves such as "preliminary increment", where a speaker says something like "Let me explain…", and points out the occurrence of "on-line amendments", where a speaker sees problems ahead in achieving a target state, and changes tack accordingly. The study of discourse has brought into prominence these two types of activity.

The first type, called a *focusing move* in Sinclair and Coulthard (1975) is part of the organisation of the discourse rather than the incrementation of shared experience; it is designed to ensure that the incrementation is successful and efficient, and so is related to the many *discourse markers* (Aijmer 2002) that are common in spoken texts. Biber et al (1999: 225) talk of discourse markers and other text signals as "non-clausal material in conversation" and show how they make a counterpoint with the increments:

> B: Well — I got it from that travel agent's
> A: Oh.
> B: er the one
> A: In the precinct?
> B: by, yeah, by Boots.
> A: Oh yeah, Boots.
>   (from Biber et al)

Biber et al point out that by a simple process of deleting the items which are not incremental, a perfectly coherent sentence emerges *I got it from the travel agent's, the one in the precinct by Boots.*[1]

Not all stretches of conversation are so amenable to this analysis, but it is a simple and insightful demonstration of one of our major distinctions, set out in Step Two (Chapter 6).

Very deep structure

At the other extreme of the linguistic spectrum from Brazil and the interactive world of discourse stands Carstairs-McCarthy, whose book on complexity (1999) is "an enquiry into the evolutionary beginnings of sentences, syllables and truth". There are obvious correspondences between the likely physiological and psychological origins of chunking, and Carstairs-McCarthy's argument linking the structure of sentences with the anatomical development of the human species. He first of all points out that human language consists of two quite different kinds of organisation, the noun phrase and the sentence; then he argues that it is not necessary for communication to have these two; one would be sufficient. So the question arises, why is the existence of these contrasting structures a universal in human language; from this the author traces the origins of language back to the developmental changes in the tongue and larynx of early man.

A supportive quote from Strawson on the back cover is particularly revealing: "…the distinction between noun phrase and sentence (and hence between refer-

---

1. Stig Johansson pointed this out to us at a Workshop

ence and truth)". Let us bypass the question of whether noun phrase and sentence are accidental or essential for the kind of communication that we are familiar with; let us also shrink from the full implications of "truth", and assume that Strawson merely wanted to point out that sentences in principle can have truth value, whereas noun phrases cannot. Nevertheless, there is an important point here which is germane to our position.

There are two kinds of organisation of words in text. One, typified by the noun phrase, is a grouping of words to make a *textual object* that participates in the construction as a single unit. Its role is to be a point of attention; it can combine with one or more other textual objects to update the virtual world of shared experience. In the case of a noun phrase it typically combines, as a subject or an object or complement, with a verb to make a clause, and the role of a clause is to update the virtual world. The clause is not the only structure which combines objects in an update, nor is the noun phrase the only kind of textual object; but the fundamental distinction runs through much linguistic thinking, from the theoretical position of Carstairs-McCarthy to the data-focused Brazil. We are happy to adopt and develop this position towards the end of the book.

Linearity

On the linearity of text we turn to Beaugrande (1984), who offers a thorough and detailed analysis, largely from the perspective of the text producer. Our focus is on the text as it is received; we do not want to engage with the production side because of all the issues it raises of motivation, planning, decision-making etc. that take place before the text assumes its outward shape. While these matters are of the utmost importance for a comprehensive understanding of language as communication, they are highly controversial at the present time, especially with swift developments in neuroscience. Since we can describe our data without having to take a stance on the way it is assembled, we can take a fairly simple view of linearity.

Beaugrande offers seven principles of linearity, all relevant to the reception side, but with varying priority. Two ("core-and-adjunct", and "heaviness") deal with the relative importance of constituents, which is an important issue in determining chunk boundaries. The "pause" principle provides valuable evidence for boundaries and the "look-ahead" principle is similar to our *prospection*. Much of the "look-back" principle deals with varieties of anaphora, it but includes the perception that a stretch of text recalls a previous stretch of text in a quasi-parallel structure; in this area it combines with the "listing" principle. The "disambiguation" principle, which excludes unwanted readings, is only required occasionally in actual practice.

Beaugrande reminds us that strict linearity is too rigid a model for the production and reception of speech and writing. In the early chapters of this book we present texts word by word, and even character by character, but this is partly for convenience and partly in order to encourage readers to appreciate text as it unfolds. From the earliest experiments of Ladefoged (Broadbent and Ladefoged 1959) seen against the background of Miller's (1956) claims for the short term memory, it has been clear that at the very outset of the interpretative process some hierarchy is imposed on the linearity of text, with a strong tendency to prioritise gestalt patterns where relevant. The notion of chunking fits well into this state of affairs.

Construction grammar

Some features of Linear Unit Grammar have been noted as similar to those of Construction Grammar (CxG; see Östman and Fried 2005). The holistic approach, the lack of a predetermined hierarchy of units into which everything has to fit, the separation of relationships external to a construction and those internal to it; these are all features that are shared at least superficially. But the differences are substantial. There is hardly any account taken of linearity in CxG, and there is a strong emphasis on hierarchy from the start, with the boxes-within-boxes diagrams that are the main organising principle of the description. Although external and internal relationships are kept separate, they are assigned in a single-cycle process; there is no "bootstrapping" element as there is in the step-by-step analysis of LUG.

Despite the avoidance of pre-specified constructions, there are very strong and pre-determined patterns of description in CxG that are applied to incoming data; both in the anticipated syntactic categories and in the semantic theory (which is independent of the syntax but is generally accepted by adherents of CxG theory) there are familiar criteria like well-formedness and argumentations of an essentially paradigmatic nature, which contrast sharply with the syntagmatic orientation of LUG.

There is also a clear difference in the aims of these approaches; CxG is committed to a comprehensive description, and its "potential for a uniform description of *all* grammatical knowledge" (op.cit: 18) is frequently asserted. This is said to include "irregular" and "exceptional" structures (quote marks Östman and Fried), and stress is laid on the breadth of coverage and the lack of central or kernel structures; however the range seems unlikely to include the varieties that are studied here. But the greatest contrast of all is that LUG makes no claim to go into anything like the kind of detail that CxG, and most other grammars, have as their main area of concentration. LUG attempts to cover hitherto inaccessible varieties, to bring them into the fold and to prepare them for the more detailed attention of conventional grammars, and in that sense CxG is a conventional grammar. LUG is neutral as to whether all the criteria used in paradigm grammars, and all the distinctions that are felt to be obligatory in an adequate description, are in fact essential to the business of showing how meaning is created by text. So LUG attempts in this present instance to be complementary rather than competitive with established grammars; the differing priorities are discussed in Chapter 12.

Linearity and syntax

Some recent models of syntax take linearity on board and invoke a left-to right approach to language (e.g. Kempson et al. 2001; O'Grady 2005). Their goals differ from ours in that they are oriented towards modelling syntax. We do not prioritise or separate syntactic structures, but take language as it comes, as holistically as we can, and segment it as it most naturally seems to fall into chunks. Despite such fundamental differences, there are also affinities between our approach and other models with a linear conceptualisation of language.

Kempson et al in their *Dynamic Syntax* (DS; 2001) present a model of natural language understanding which takes the interpretation of a language string to be constructed incrementally from left to right. Like LUG, DS puts priority on the hearer's/reader's viewpoint. DS proposes a formal, rule-based model of the parsing process and argues that syntactic core phenomena can be explained on the basis of the way in which representations of content are incrementally built up. DS thus prioritises semantic interpretation over syntactic; it also makes reference to general pragmatic operations, implying underdetermination of full logical forms for grammar. The model observes perceptively that interpretative processes need to work on incomplete units most of the time — apart from the very end of a string. In this way, the parsing process must operate dynamically as a sequence of successively richer descriptions of a form of the unfolding sentence.

It is definitely a strength in this model that it recognises the need for processing to be dynamic and operate on incomplete data. However, the notion of 'completeness' in DS is based on syntactic well-formedness. This works well as long as we operate entirely within the limits of individual 'well-formed' sentences. DS does exactly this, and therefore it misses out on the possibility of structural units continuing past completion. The difference can be illustrated with their own (contrived) example (Kempson et al 2001: 4), *John upset Mary*. In circumstances which are just as plausible as the utterance of this sentence, the example could be expanded into *John upset Mary by telling us about it*, or continued even further (e.g. *John upset Mary by telling us about it first*) without affecting the completeness of the structure. Any of these sentences can be regarded as complete, but whether they are finished can only be determined on the basis of what follows in the text as we move from left to right; if a new structure is begun, the first one must be regarded as finished. Structures thus have completion points, which need not put an end to the hearer's task of processing a given string until it is finished. Speakers appear to be able to make a distinction between complete and finished — finishing being recognised by the beginning of a new incomplete structure. This distinction is built into the approach described in this book (see Chapter 11).

DS is intended as an account of interpreting natural language by assigning a logical form, i.e. a tree structure, on it. In practice, natural language data in the sense of attested examples do not come into the picture. Kempson et al. start off promisingly by talking about online processing:

> Knowing a language means being able to segment sounds in that language into units, recover information from those units, and use this information to work out what someone communicating in that language has intended to convey. (Kempson et al. 2001: 1)

This is what they refer to as the "common-sense view of language", which they wish to adopt as their point of departure. This suggests that they seek to account for natural language as it is encountered by a hearer. However, their analysis uses only written sentences. Although Kempson et al. do not discuss the distinction between spoken and written language, their model seems to try to capture the processing of sentences heard. This is not a happy solution because spoken language is not organised in terms of sentences and written language is not heard.

O'Grady in his *Syntactic Carpentry* (2005) presents a more radical departure from traditional syntax. His model is intended to replace grammar in favour of a processing-based model of syntax. In practice his emergentist theory of language structure nevertheless focuses on syntax, and a central concern of his is the description of syntactic dependency resolution.

In line with emergentism, O'Grady posits that the processing mechanisms of language are similar to or based on more general properties of the cognitive system, thus not specific to syntax. His ultimate aim is therefore to reduce the theory of sentence structure to the theory of sentence processing. For this end, he postulates a computational system which consists of an efficiency driven linear processor handling the processing of syntactic dependencies. The basic idea is that the design of a sentence reflects the way it is built; the processing system seeks to resolve dependencies at the first opportunity, working in a linear order and processing one word at a time.

The left to right processing is not to be understood quite literally, though, because the processor does not begin to operate from the first element it encounters but from the first verb. As soon as there is a verb, the processor can resort to argument resolution which operates essentially from left to right.

Both Kempson et al. and O'Grady assume that syntactic processing works on one word at a time. It seems more plausible, however, that in practice linguistic processing is more schema-based, and that fluent speakers neither construct nor interpret language by first breaking it down into its minimal independent components. As many researchers from psycholinguistic and conversational studies have pointed out (see e.g. Bybee and Hopper 2001; N.Ellis 2003; Wray 2002), speakers are likely to store multiple representations of items in memory. In this way they are capable of using the 'same' items in novel combinations as well as in larger conventional units; well-entrenched composite items are an important part of both production and comprehension. These account for a considerable part of speaker fluency. While it may well be that speakers are capable of breaking down syntactic structures into their component parts and thus getting down to word level, it is not likely that their understanding of language in use hinges upon this.

DS draws on cognitive science, especially the representational theory of mind, and focuses on the interpretative process to the exclusion of production. Yet it makes little reference to empirical work on processing. In contrast, O'Grady makes ample reference to empirical psycholinguistic findings — but all of these are based on measurements of subjects processing contrived, isolated written sentences in laboratory conditions. While such studies may well reveal something about people's intuitions about syntactic structure, they are not very illuminating as regards using language in natural circumstances.

A fundamental distinction between these linear models of syntax and our approach is that unlike us, these models do not take attested language data as their point of departure. They operate on variants of invented sentences in isolation. Basically our model need not be incompatible with such accounts of syntactic structure, but since our point of departure is in discourse, we take on board phenomena which are ignored by sentence-based models. Sentences are not central to our analysis because they are not taken as primitives; where relevant they come up at a much later stage.

Intonation and talk

The limited capacity of the working memory has found its way to many recent linguistic models which are not in themselves part of a psycholinguistic or cognitive tradition (e.g. Mukherjee 2001; O'Grady 2005). This is undoubtedly a welcome development in bringing together previously largely separate perspectives on language structure, but it needs to be kept in mind that the capacity of the working memory is not as clearly determinable as it is sometimes made out to be. Miller's (1956) classic model, where 'short-term memory' consists of seven chunks, has been developed and challenged in many ways, even though it still seems to have a strong foothold in working memory research. The size and nature of the chunks that are being processed appear to affect memory capacity, for example to what extent lexical items have familiar contents (Hulme et al. 1995). Cowan (2001), in turn, has proposed that only four chunks take up all the space.

Thus, while it seems to be generally accepted that the working memory is of limited capacity, the precise implications of this cannot be stated with much certainty or precision. Most models are happy to refer to the limits, but the precise capacity is not known. The actual neural basis of working memory is largely unknown, and there may not be a special module or centre allocated for this. It may also be useful to keep in mind that simplicity and elegance in a model need not match what the brain actually does. As Paradis (2004: 33) points out, the brain in general has been shown to favour redundancy rather than economy in its functioning.

Limited processing capacity is invoked in some models which assume intonation as the basis of segmentation. Chafe's (1994, 2006) "intonation units" and Mukherjee's (2001) "talk units" take intonation as the basis of their speech chunks. Chafe makes use of a number of different criteria in determining the boundaries of his intonation units — pauses, acceleration, pitch level, pitch contours among others — and the interpretation of a unit boundary is where any or all of these features are present (see Chafe 1994: 58–60). This relates in an interesting way to Abney's φ-phrases units (discussed in the section on partial parsing above). If many features converge at the same point, a boundary assignment seems quite convincing; at the same time the procedure leaves plenty of room for variable assignment of boundaries. Chafe seeks to determine units of processing by this segmentation, with the ultimate aim of understanding the flow of consciousness and speaking in one holistic theory. This is a more ambitious goal than ours in this book. We are more modestly aiming at bringing linear text and grammar closer to each other, and observing the consequences of this to the understanding of language.

What is also interesting for us in Chafe's work here is that he goes on to classify the intonation units into three main types: substantive, regulatory and fragmentary. The substantive units convey ideas of events, states, or referents, and the regulatory units regulate interaction or information flow, and largely coincide with discourse markers. Units which seem to be truncated are called fragmentary (Chafe 1994: 63).

Chafe's functional categories are not unlike the types of chunks we find, but since our assignment of boundaries takes place on a different basis to begin with, the consequent functional analyses diverge as well. So for example Chafe's functional assignments can lead to the three main unit types appearing simultaneously at different levels: units of one kind can be included in units of another kind. For example, the segment *her she has an enlarged heart* is a substantive unit, but the beginning shows the speaker's change of mind after the first word; so *her* would seem to fit the category 'fragmentary' because it is not followed up. In Linear Unit

Grammar, we do not subsume fragments under other units. Nevertheless, Chafe's units are interesting and have the distinct advantage of being based on observing recorded language use in context, not invented examples or isolated sentences presented to subjects in laboratory conditions.

Mukherjee (2001) analyses 'talk units' at the intersection of syntax and intonation, thus adding an angle and a basis of segmentation in comparison to Chafe. He builds on Halford's (1996) earlier work on 'talk units'. Mukherjee looks at tone units and syntax; talk units are 'presentation structures', as he calls them, whose boundaries are determined by the interplay of the two levels. Syntactic and tonal closure vs. openness constitute the basic variables, and by observing their interaction, Mukherjee manages to generate interesting hypotheses about information packaging, text typological differences and turn-taking.

Unlike many studies on similar issues, Mukherjee tests his hypotheses on a sample of transcribed speech. Like us, he emphasises the local nature of speech structuring, taking notice of Brazil's (1995) thesis concerning the incremental nature of speech, and points out that parasyntactic structures are "not planned by the speaker from the outset, but rather incrementally in the course of speech production and on the basis of local decisions" (Mukherjee 2001: 104). He combines insights from linguistics, particularly functionalist traditions, both Hallidayan and 'axiomatic functionalism' (see Mulder 1989), with brain research findings on working memory. This is a useful step towards capturing the complex interactions of components in spoken language. Clearly, speakers and hearers must process simultaneously much more than intonation and syntax, but isolating components to form a simple and testable model helps us make sense of some of the facets of this complex process.

Although Mukherjee's model has certain affinities with ours, there are also important differences. On the whole, we do not isolate any strands or levels of language for our particular focus, but take the ongoing language stream as it comes. The only thing we abstract ourselves from is the actual sound, since we only occasionally consult the soundtrack of the speech extracts, and this only post hoc, to settle points of uncertainty. In fact, in doing this we do not differ much from Mukherjee, who does not work on sound either, although the transcripts he uses are much narrower than any of ours. Most importantly, however, we proceed in a highly data-driven way, and avoid predetermined linguistic categories. We engage in intuition-based chunking with as many boundary insertions as we feel comfortable with, and continue our analysis from there. The outcomes of the segmenting procedures of Mukherjee's and our model diverge; we place boundaries in different places, as might be expected.

Unlike either Chafe or Mukherjee, we take as our point of departure a speaker's intuitive, implicit recognition of a potential boundary. We do not start from a complex set of objective measurements and then try to match the result with an analyst's or speaker's subjective perception of the units afterwards; we begin from the simple perception of boundaries and work our way towards categorisation and greater complexity very gradually, in fact leaving complex relations like syntactic dependencies to models specialising in those.

Processing

Humans chunk incoming information as part of their normal perceptual processes. We learn perceptual skills by gradually developing schemata which guide our perception, and which undergo changes and adjustments in our interaction with reality (see e.g. Neisser 1980). Our schemata help us chunk information in a meaningful way. The term 'chunk' was suggested by Miller (1956) in his seminal work on short-term memory, to which we have already made reference several times. Chunking forms a connection between perception and learning, as repeated chunks get entrenched in memory.

The effective chunking of incoming information was widely utilised in the teaching of reading in the 1970s and the 1980s, much influenced by schema theory (Rumelhart 1980; Smith 1978). Working memory has limited capacity, but by grouping incoming information we can make it handle more material than by attending to the smallest units possible. This process of chunking when faced with a stream of language is essentially linear, even though the discussions on teaching reading laid much emphasis on the possibility of going back and forth in written text. Yet in order to make sense of a stretch of text, it is necessary to go through it in a linear fashion at least once quite independently of how many times one might want to go back to check things for accuracy or for better understanding.

For spoken language, linearity is generally accepted as a necessary and constitutive feature. Levelt's (1989) influential psycholinguistic model of speech is strictly built on the basis of on-line 'left-to-right' processing, modularity, and parallel processing. It is an 'incremental' model in the sense that individual components (such as the 'conceptualizer' or the 'articulator'), which operate in parallel, each work on fragments of the type of input they specialise in. Both incrementality and parallel processing are crucial to fluency according to Levelt. That neurological processing occurs in parallel is also commonly accepted in more recent accounts (see e.g. Dąbrowska 2004). An interesting consequence of this incremental parallel processing is that, as Levelt points out,

> there is no single unit of talk. Different processing components have their own characteristic processing units, and these may or may not be preserved in the articulatory pattern of speech. (Levelt 1989: 24)

If speech is processed in different kinds of unit fragments in the production stages, it is likely to lead to different kinds of chunks in output and in comprehension. It is therefore plausible that an intuitive chunking exercise based on an extended sequence of words will lead to units which on closer inspection turn out to be of several different kinds. This is what happens in applying the linear model we are presenting. Postulating parallel and non-coextensive processing for different components is also reflected in "staggered" segmentation between syntagms and prosodic units, observed in simultaneous analyses of syntax and prosody (Esser, 1998; Mukherjee 2001). Pausing in spontaneous speech often does not occur at clause boundaries, which is further support for the interpretation that there is no neat co-extension in language processing by different components.

While it is clear that speech production and reception are not mirror images of each other, it is equally clear that they must share many characteristics on the basis of their on-line orientation under temporal constraints. Conversation is also interactive throughout, and it is hard to imagine that rapid turn-taking, cooperative construction or collaborative completion would be possible if the mechanisms of production and reception were radically different; in reality, changes between the roles of speaker and hearer are generally smooth. In addition to completing each other's turns, speakers are also capable of monitoring their own speech, which would seem to suggest relatively similar simultaneous processes.

The widely acknowledged problem of accounting for the processing of complex structures and processing under real-time constraints has been challenged by those who approach language from the perspective of social interaction. For example Laury (2006) shows that seemingly complex structures can be simple to process for interactants who employ familiar, predictable and largely routinised structural units; speakers' ability to form complex sentences originates in knowledge about social interaction, such as ways of presenting referents and evaluating them. Recurrent situation types give rise to certain linguistic structures, which in turn strengthen the structures, and together these processes result in grammatical routines.

Work by scholars who emphasise social interaction in the shaping of grammar (e.g. Bybee 2005; Ford et al 2003; DuBois 2003; Couper-Kuhlen and Seltin 2001; Schegloff et al. 1996) are compatible with our approach. While we attempt no analysis of the social context of our data, we believe that the use of natural language in interaction is fundamental to the ways in which grammars are shaped, and that the processing of language in ongoing conversation is geared towards interaction. Data which is most likely to take linguistic research forward is that which is recorded in interaction. This is not to deny that written text is interactive, but it manifests its interactive nature in ways which are not the same as those of speech.

As speakers chunk incoming information to make it more manageable, they also observe recurrences in its sequences, and make meaningful associations between recurrent sequences and other states of affairs. The sequences which recur get stored in (long-term) memory. It seems that in the initial stages of first language acquisition and natural second language acquisition we acquire unanalysed chunks, but that these gradually get broken down into smaller components (cf. e.g. N. Ellis 1996, 2003; McLaughlin 1987; Wong Fillmore 1979; Wray 2002). The components then become available for forming new combinations, while the originally acquired larger schemata are also stored in memory. As Dąbrowska puts it (2004: 200): ". . . development proceeds from invariant formulas through increasingly general formulaic frames to abstract templates."

Adult speakers then possess multiple representations of items in their linguistic repertoire: as part of schematic or formulaic wholes, and as units capable of entering into new combinations (see e.g. Bybee and Hopper 2001; Wray 2002). The prefabricated chunks are utilised in fluent output, which, as many researchers from different traditions have noted, largely depends on automatic processing of stored units. According to Erman and Warren's (2000) count, about half of running text is covered by such recurrent units.

Some scholars also suggest that units which are not merely routines of verbatim repetitions, but contain variable elements as well, are likely to constitute basic units of processing (Bybee 2003; Wray 2002). Constructions in Construction Grammar are an example of the latter kind of unit.

As Dąbrowska points out (2004: 24), most prefabricated units are fairly small: between two and three words. Therefore psychologically realistic grammars must accommodate both complex and simple units. What this adds up to is a repertoire of small units which are invariable routines, small units which are partly variable, and combinations of these in larger and more complex units — and all of these need to be processed somehow to compose fluent speech and comprehension in ongoing interaction. In all, it seems that accepting more than one kind of processing unit is fairly realistic. It also seems likely that grammars which are based on shallow parsing are more likely to handle this successfully than those in which deep and complex preplanning is postulated.

There has been a good deal of interest in elements which are "between the word and the clause" (Stubbs 1996), but which do not occupy a definite constituent status in traditional grammatical models. Most of this interest has emphasised the recurrent nature of such units in speech and text, either as invariant routines or with some variable elements as part of the unit. Many names have been used for them: prefabs, lexical bundles, fixed expressions, formulaic sequences, etc. They tend to be conceptualised as lexis-centred units, that is, be built around a lexical item and its accompanying elements. They are generally seen as alternatives to rule-based models of language, and share something of Becker's formulation:

> Suppose that, instead of shaping discourse according to rules, one really pulls old language from memory (particular old language, with all its words in and everything) and then reshapes it to current context. (Becker 1983: 218)

Recurrent chunks of language constitute important units of meaning (Sinclair 2004), and they have been recognised in recent grammars to an extent. Biber et al (1999) talk about 'lexical bundles' which in effect are subsets of n-grams. A more formal and theoretically ambitious account, Construction Grammar (see Fillmore et al. 1988; Östman and Fried 2005; and the discussion earlier in this chapter) is a formal grammar based on constructions which comprise both lexical and structural elements. Pragmatic routines are often based on recurrent chunks (Aijmer 1996). The concept of the recurrent chunk, often with an emphasis on its invariant aspects, has also become the basis of a good deal of work on second language acquisition (Nattinger and DeCarrico 1992; Hakuta 1976; Wong and Fillmore 1979; N. Ellis 2002, 2003).

Our interest in this book is in not in the recurrent aspect of chunks, but in the other dimension, that of the tendency of speakers and listeners to chunk language into manageable units as they participate in language-mediated interaction. Are we dealing with the same units from two perspectives, that is, do these chunks coincide? Not necessarily. Linear chunking which aids perception and sense making in ongoing discourse provides material for abstraction which ensues from recurrent encounters of the same or similar expressions, but does not need to correspond to the boundaries of units which are conventionalised or whose recurrence is meaningful.

In this book, we approach chunking in the basic sense of sorting incoming information, and do not pay attention to the recurrent features of the chunks themselves, be they invariant or variable. We assume the perspective of linear processing, and utilise our own capacity for chunking up language. Clearly, the flow of language we are dealing with is of a peculiar kind, because it is transcribed speech (and in some cases written language), and we have looked at it word by word, with the transcription already giving us the words. Nevertheless, when we have made essentially intuitive boundary marking, we have been falling back on our sense of a 'natural' boundary. So, ours is a research method which makes use of this ability to chunk, obviously not pretending to simulate the online processing of speech but making use of the more general intuitive capacity. The further steps in our analysis are more traditional in that we posit categories with functional distinctions and test the hypothetical cases on data, refining and modifying them on the basis of the data.

CHAPTER 3

Data description

The data in this book is a selection of extracts from several different types of discourse. The sampling has been done in a manner which resembles usual practices in qualitative research methods, even though this was not a clear initial plan. We began with one extract of spoken language and worked out a preliminary framework on the basis of that. When we had agreed that the system worked on this extract, we went on to test it on another extract, then a third, adjusting and developing the system as we went along. Rather than re-sample from the same variety, we tried to extend the range of varieties with each sample.

We first focused on extracts of transcribed speech, and then added a sample of highly compressed written language. When we felt satisfied with the method of analysis, the question arose as to whether it would work on ordinary written language as well. Since written language normally presents few problems to conventional grammatical analysis because it is what grammars have been constructed on, it may seem slightly superfluous for us to include samples of that variety. Yet applying this speech-based system to written data provided an interesting test of its power. In all, the process has been fundamentally data-driven, making use of intuition at the outset but developing the analytical system from a simple set of preliminary assumptions by applying it successively to data samples and adjusting it to account for each sample. Since the objective was to build a model rather than account for a specific set of data, say, a genre or some other principled collection of texts, we cast our nets wide and sampled extracts as diverse as we could think of.

All the extracts were chosen primarily on text-external criteria: we wanted diversity and we wanted to capture texts which at the outset might be considered unusual from a normative point of view. The reason was to ensure robustness for the evolving model. After getting each text we chose an extract which seemed to have a beginning and an end in dealing with a topic. In practice we had to cut down the extracts further as we went along, because they were far too long to be presentable in an analysis although they looked short enough before being analysed. All texts are authentic in that they have not been produced in experimental conditions or for this research but have occurred spontaneously.

Sample 1, Lexis

The first text, which we call "Lexis" is a transcription of spoken dialogue for computer processing. The transcript is of one of the first recordings made for a spoken language corpus, dating from 1963. It is the first item in the selection from the corpus that is held in the Oxford Text Archive http://www.ota.ox.ac.uk/texts/0173.html and is freely downloadable. The corpus is described in detail in Krishnamurthy (ed.) 2004.

The original soundtrack is lost, and all we have is this upper-case rendering of the dialogue, using just 26 letters and the space key. Speaker change is not marked, neither are any paralinguistic features. The original transcription was made using the conventions of the day, and would have looked like a playscript, with speaker change marked; in most cases one of the participants was able to review the transcript and help with speaker identification. It is still possible that the original transcription will be found. When the data was prepared for computer input, it was decided to strip off everything but the words which had been uttered; this was partly to facilitate lexical analysis, which had not been attempted before, and partly because of a growing conviction that the continuous text had a status of its own.

The recording was made in Edinburgh, and the participants were students of the University and their friends. All were native speakers of English. The conversation took place in a coffee room which was under the control of the corpus project team and which was specially adapted for making efficient recordings of conversations. The speakers gathered for coffee in a pleasant room; no attempt was made to disguise the fact that the conversation might be recorded in the course of a linguistic experiment, but there was no obvious recording equipment on view.

Sample 2, ELFA

The second extract ("ELFA") is from the ELFA corpus (http://www.uta.fi/laitokset/kielet/engf/research/elfa/). All participants are non-native speakers of English who use English as a lingua franca. The setting is a seminar discussion at the University of Tampere, in an international MA program run in English. The discussion follows one student's presentation, which is not included in the extract. The subject is political science, the seminar participants, 10 in all, come from five different language backgrounds: Finnish, Lithuanian, Dutch, Russian and German. The extracts includes contributions from three student participants, one of whom has just given a presentation; the others ask questions and discuss the points she made.

The transcription is broad and normalised to the extent that it allows ordinary corpus search methods to be used. The idea has been to transcribe the speech in a broad and orthographically normalising manner but to keep the soundtrack available for closer scrutiny of particular episodes as needed. The original soundtrack was thus available to us and was consulted, but only at a late stage in the process of description.

Sample 3, HKCSE

The third text called the *Hong Kong Corpus of Spoken English* (HKCSE) is from a spoken corpus compiled over the period 1996-2001 at the Polytechnic University of Hong Kong, by a team led by Professors Martin Warren and Winnie Cheng. The text comes from transcript no. C113, which is a conversation in a restaurant, between two women. One is a native speaker of British English, and the other a Hong Kong Chinese speaker of English as a second language. The occasion is informal, discussing an upcoming party, and the speakers know each other very well; the recording was made in 1999.

The corpus consists of intercultural language use. The extract is a dialogue between a native and a non-native speaker of English. This extract was chosen for us by the corpus compilers, who did not know what our evolving analytical system was like. The original soundtrack was not initially available to us, but when we wanted to check our analysis against it, we consulted the compilers.

The speech extracts were transcribed in different ways, as can be expected given their temporal and geographical distance. We did not want to change them just for the sake of uniformity, especially as we did not always have access to the sound and alterations would have been too risky. One thing we did change, though, was the laughter signals, which we also removed from the ELFA extract because the first transcript (*Lexis*) did not mark laughter. This means information loss, because laughter plays an important role in interaction. We maintained other markers like hesitations (*erm*) and backchannelling (*mhm*), and it could be argued that drawing the line here is arbitrary. So it is, but the line is bound to be arbitrary in transcribing real interactive speech; we made the choice because we did not have similar information from the other extracts.

Sample 4, *The Independent*

After completing the spoken analysis, we wanted to test the model with a text which, unlike the extracts so far, was as 'normal' as possible. We turned to written language, and chose an U.K. broadsheet newspaper editorial. The selection criterion was that it should correspond to our notion of the prototypical newspaper editorial. The extract named "Independent" is from the *Independent* newspaper for July 19, 2005, and is part of an editorial titled "Charles Kennedy must live up to his words". It is a comment on domestic politics in the UK, the traditional territory of editorials.

We satisfied ourselves that the normal text complied with the model, and decided to explore the written medium a little more, to see whether more exotic written text could also be handled in the same way.

Sample 5, Joyce

One text was chosen from the literary domain, because a recurrent criticism of linguistic models is that they fail to account for literary text; obviously aesthetic values cannot be captured like this, but it is a reasonable test for an analytical model to see whether it can be applied to a literary text. There is a huge range of literary writing, and we did not want to choose an easy sample, so we settled on James Joyce, the acknowledged master of putting words into the mouths of his characters. The extract "Joyce" is from the opening of the final section of *Ulysses* (www.online-literature.com/ james_joyce/ ulysses/18/). Section 18, *Penelope*) is 24,199 words in length and almost without punctuation, apparently uttered by one of the characters, Molly Bloom. Our passage occurs near the beginning of the section.

Sample 6, Gazetteer

The third sample of written prose was taken from the highly compressed English of reference manuals. The extract was actually introduced into the study at midstage, but it has been left to the end because it has features of a highly specialised text, which are not shared by the others, not even the Joyce passage. *Gazetteer* is a text type which is frequent enough in anyone's experience, but rarely chosen for analysis. Although familiar, texts of this type rarely attract interest apart from the information they convey. The extract is from an encyclopaedia, one of those texts we tend to "see through" rather than dwell on the unusual aspects of their structure. It is highly compressed, abbreviated language of the kind which is common in reference books. Pears Cyclopedia was first published in 1897, and our extract is taken from the 97th edition. The Gazetteer is 182 pages long, comprising Section K of the book, in between J – Ideas and Beliefs, and L – General Information

It is written text, in a variety of compressed English that mark it out as unusual compared with ordinary written prose. Various kinds of compression of text have always been part of the written form, from scribes and stonemasons seeking economy of labour, through the early days of the telegraph to the texters of today. It is clearly a property of a language that it lends itself to certain kinds of compression when the circumstances require it.

This text became relevant to our enquiry when, after some trials, we began to feel that LUG was not only appropriate for the description of transcribed conversations, but for a wide range of texts that were beyond the scope of existing grammars. In the case of this text, there was solid proof of the lamentable performance of conventional grammars on it; one of us (JS) had already published a short paper raising the topic and using this text as part of the exemplar (Sinclair 1988). Since clause structure, as normally treated, is determined principally by the choice of verb, the results of applying such a grammar to a variety of English with no finite verbs, and precious few verbs of any kind, were unedifying.

The text is in English, however abbreviated. Many of the most noticeable features of English are absent, and no doubt it could be "translated" into German or French with only minor adjustment, but it is a variety of English and therefore it should be describable with a grammar of English. Unfortunately, the tactic of any grammar that took on the task of describing such a text would be to re-write it first, expanded into neat, clean sentences which could then be analysed.

Obviously, these six extracts do not attempt to cover all important types of text. Their selection does not result from any systematic sampling procedure planned in advance in search of representativeness. They simply reflect as wide a variety as was needed for a reasonable saturation point. The objective was to develop and test a model to a point at which it is sketched out sufficiently for further work and other analysts.

Section B

Analysis

CHAPTER 4

System of analysis

In this chapter, we introduce the analytical system which will be developed in the next five chapters (Chapters 5 to 9). Here we present the outline of our approach and its position relative to existing models of grammar. The provenance and scope of LUG are discussed, before going into more depth and detail in the rest of the book.

Provenance and scope

Any sequence of alphanumeric characters is acceptable as input to this system of analysis; so any written or printed text, or orthographic transcript of a spoken language event can be analysed. There is no *linguistic* requirement on a text other than that it is a record of a communicative event (and in our case purports to be in English).

This starting point may seem unremarkable, but it stands in sharp contrast with the kinds of structural analysis of text that are characteristic of the linguistic disciplines. In traditional analysis, before instrumentation, only certain sentences were deemed capable of analysis; prescriptive criteria like "correctness", followed by quasi-descriptive criteria such as "grammaticalness" and "well-formedness" were used somewhat tautologically — i.e. only those sentences which fitted the grammar could be satisfactorily described. This in effect sets up a fitness test for each sentence before it could be admitted into the grammar; inevitably this requirement has been clouded in uncertainty.

Despite remarkable developments in linguistic theory and description over the last half-century, the situation has not improved greatly. The study of spoken discourse has added some new categories and classes, but, as we shall see, these form more of a parallel development than an integral one. Most of the purely grammatical research has gone into achieving greater precision among established structural patterns, and greater generality across languages.

In computationally-based analysis there is now a requirement of explicitness in the description of structures in an algorithm or computer program, and this exposes the flexibility that was taken for granted in pre-computing days. Since all participants in a session of analysis are highly accomplished speakers of at least one language, it has been normal to rely on intuitive leaps. As a consequence there is little or no pressure on linguists to adopt scientific rigour or even to define terms strictly. Language teachers and learners do not put pressure on the grammarians to be more explicit because they share the ability to intuit what they need. They find it easier to adjust their intuitive categories to the partial descriptions rather than demand fully explicit description, which would be intellectually very demanding.

The computer does not make intuitive leaps, and it punishes the slightest lack of clarity in a description. Of necessity any naturally-occurring text has to be *preprocessed* until it fits the description — the machine equivalent of well-formedness, but much more limited because it is finite. It is unlikely even now that ordinary specimens of apparently well-formed text (i.e. specimens giving no difficulty to human-based analysis) can be adequately described by existing programs.

A Linear Unit Grammar is not a preprocessor, but it overlaps in function while working on entirely different principles. LUG takes fairly raw data and knocks it into shape for input to a conventional grammar, developing it from problematic material to something close to well-formedness. In contrast, preprocessing is essentially a kind of complex proof-reading which aims at naturalising the text to arbitrary conventions of the analytic process. It is not principled and it is essentially manual although sometimes machine-assisted. In contrast LUG is systematic and replicable; it does not occupy an uneasy position between the data and the grammar because it provides the basis on which the grammar will be built.

The provenance and scope of LUG, then, can be judged with reference to the practice of preprocessing. The minimum amount of disruption is done to the linear sequence of textual events, and one possible use of the output, which is discussed later (Chapter 11) would be as input to a hierarchical grammar — or rather, to a grammar, since they are all hierarchical.

LUG is presented here as the application of speakers' spontaneous internalised perceptions, and as dependent on intuitive responses to complex data. It looks at first sight unlikely that much of the analysis could be replicated on a computer, yet the method outlined here is heavily procedural, and towards the end of the book (Chapter 12) we address the possibility of automating some or all of the analysis.

Step-by-step analysis

The experience of text is a very rich one, and to someone who knows the language well it is a holistic event; it is almost impossible to isolate individual features and examine them thoroughly. Superimposing a complex structural model would certainly endanger intuitive responses to the data, and our method relies heavily on intuitive responses from the analyst. So we decided on a model of successive steps, each of which is simple in itself. We chose to present the analysis as a series of questions, each simple, direct and complete in itself, with only a small number of alternative answers. No account is taken of later steps while one is being implemented, nor of previous steps beyond the one that forms the input data for the step. A first-order Markov model fits the step-by-step analysis that we propose.

Step 1

The first step is to assign Provisional Unit Boundaries (PUBs) to a chosen text. This, we claim, is the harnessing of an intuitive perception of users of a language, and they can without effort divide the text satisfactorily. By "satisfactorily" is meant with reasonable consistency one with another, though we must expect that some individual variation is likely to occur, and some cases are likely to remain doubtful.

At this stage we try to make the task as intuitive as possible, offering no rules and very little guidance. The only specific advice we offer, arising from our own previous experience, is that in cases of doubt it is preferable to introduce a boundary. This is also of practical value because it is easy later on to erase unnecessary boundaries, but it is less easy to introduce new ones. Although this stage is the one which is most vulnerable to misunderstanding and muddle, we have experienced very few problems, and conclude that it is a reasonable first step in analysis.

The PUBs indicate the *chunks* of text that form the input to the next step. A chunk is any stretch of text that is bounded by a PUB on either side[1].

Step 2

The second step is to classify each of the provisional units into one of two varieties — the incremental and the organisational. We assume that the purpose and intent of a conversation or a document is to increment shared experience, and that many of the chunks serve this purpose. In early models of communication it was often claimed that there was a discernible "message", which was encoded in the text, and was decoded by the hearer. This is a convenient notion and most popular ways of talking about language seem to take it for granted. However, it trivialises the notion of communication, and we do not subscribe to the idea that the message is somehow distinct from the language carrying it. Nevertheless we do ask of each successive unit, whether or not it focuses on the subject matter that is being talked about, leading to the incrementation of shared experience.

---

1. This is not a general definition of a chunk; in the Introduction we decline to define a chunk because we regard it as a pre-theoretical notion; this is a guide to its practical identification within a Linear Unit Grammar, and because it relies on the meaning of a PUB it has no value outside LUG.

If a unit is clearly not oriented towards the incrementation of shared experience, then it must be oriented towards enabling this process of incrementation, that is to say, the management of the communication. The issues of management differ markedly from one situation to another, with informal conversation at one extreme and formal written prose at the other. Nevertheless, the process of incrementation has to be managed, and there is a fundamental distinction in the functions of communicative units.

On some, thankfully rare, occasions, the distinction between orientation towards incrementation vs. management is not so easy to make. For example if a conversation is very fragmented, it may be difficult to decide on occasion what kind of unit might have been realised if a turn had been allowed to develop a little more. It is not very often that the interpretation of the text in one way rather than another hinges upon these choices, but it is possible that it makes a difference. Sometimes these issues can be resolved by consulting evidence external to the text itself, for example a sound recording of a speech event. But these may not be available or decisive, and if so, the case remains unresolved.

A few cases of this kind are highlighted in the detailed application of the analytical system that follows this introduction. But it must be emphasised that interpreting a text involves something of a clarification process: as speakers process a spoken or written text, they quickly work out the meaning, but are usually unable to recall the actual wording afterwards, let alone intonation contours, pauses etc. Moreover, not every detail of a communicative event is as relevant as any other to the value of that event as an incrementation of shared experience, so there is some prioritisation, maybe also summarisation of some kind. In any case it is clear that the text is undergoing fast and heavy processing as it unfolds, and the limitations of the working memory alone prevent us from retaining the exact form of utterances spoken or heard. We can also cope with noise, mumbling, and inaccurate hearing; transcribers know from experience that not everything can be heard, but meaning-making is still possible.

Thus the process of interpretation is able to survive some uncertainty of realisation. This position is in marked contrast to the underlying assumption of traditional analysis, that it should be exhaustive. LUG is detailed, and ignores nothing in the alphanumeric string that is remotely relevant; but it does not strive for total explicitness, or entirely doubt-free categorisation, and in that quality we claim that our analysis is closer to representing what happens in real-life communication than the performance of descriptive systems which deal with the doubtful areas by not admitting them into the analytical arena.

At the end of this step each chunk is classified as either organisational (O) or (message)-incremental (M). The chunks are now identified as having a structural role, so from now on they are mainly referred to as *elements* of structure.

Step 3

This step concerns only the elements that have been identified in Step Two as primarily devoted to organisation and management, and it further divides them into two sub-types according to the kind of management that they focus on. The choice is between the management of an interaction, real or imaginary, and the maintenance of coherence among the incremental elements.

There are uncertainties here as well, more subtle than before, because the two sub-types use similar means of expression or make a contribution to both types of management simultaneously; in the latter case it is sometimes difficult to decide which function is uppermost. But as before, there are few cases where the decision is critical from an interpretative point of view.

Step 4

The input to this step is also the output of Step Two, but this time it is the incremental elements that are further classified. At this point we are approaching the surface richness of language, and as subtler distinctions are required, the analyst comes under pressure to keep adding new categories. This is a recognised weakness of all but the most formal grammars, because it reduces the power of prospection of the grammar, and if not resisted it turns a grammatical exercise into one of labelling. We have kept the number of categories strictly to the minimum required by the data without distorting it. At this stage of subtlety, we see also the possibility of allowing categories to form combinations. This is less weakening on the explanatory potential of the grammar than a plethora of different categories, but is recognised as another way of increasing the number of options, and it must be carefully controlled.

Most of the decisions have to do with how self-standing an element is, and if it is not self-standing, how it is to be related to another element which will complement it. Much discourse, especially conversation, shows the exigencies of real-time interaction in frequent alternation of M and O elements, whether completed or not; for a non participant observer to reconstruct the coherence of the interchange is not easy. This step, like the others, guides us in the labelling of the elements as they occur in linear sequence, with implications for what happens next but without reliance on it.

Step 5

The initial PUBs are now classified according to one basic division, and to further subdivisions within those categories. Step Five offers a procedure for reducing the original text into a reasonably coherent, reasonably "well-formed" string, which has removed those features of the original text which were exclusively concerned with the interaction, and recombined the fragmented incremental elements into units which might well be acceptable input into conventional grammars. Step Five accepts as input the combined output of Steps Three and Four, that is to say, the fully subcategorised string of elements, and is in itself a series of several small steps whose sequence is important.

The form of the final output is a linear text with two parallel annotation streams. One of these preserves the distinction made at Step Two, so that there is an outline categorisation into alternating incremental units and managing units, and the other is a set of notes on any matters which are not recognised in the categorisation.

The primary analysis into a succession of Linear Units of Meaning (LUMs) is designed to approach convergence with received units of analysis like clauses, though the mapping may not be exact in all cases with all grammars. One aim of LUG is to achieve broad compatibility with the commonly-used hierarchical analytic units, but we do not attempt an exact fit. This caveat is necessary partly because there is a wide variety of different models of received grammar, but also because we do not have enough faith that the categories of received grammar are, in general, sufficiently motivated by the data to have their structure and organisation imposed on the data that we are studying.

There is a clear contrast between, on the one hand, the very limited selection of categories and their orderly progression in normal written prose, and on the other hand the rich variety of categories in fast informal talk, and their sometimes frenetic alternation. It can be seen in this contrast that conventional grammars are remarkably insensitive to the patterns with which we are working, so there is no reason to believe that they will always happen to achieve a good match with ours. Our brief is to describe the data with a system of analysis that encompasses most of the manifestations of English, not to shore up grammars that cannot cope with the texts. Nevertheless, the boundaries are relevant to conventional analysis and should mostly co-incide with familiar boundaries. The categories identified as LUMs should be coherent units, capable of being reconciled with the categories of a conventional grammar.

CHAPTER 5

Step 1: Provisional Unit Boundaries

The previous chapter gave an overview of the system of analysis which we offer in this book. This chapter begins to explicate the system in detail. An important feature of our analytical system is that it is applied in stages, that is, one operation at a time. The detailed presentation of how it works is therefore best shown in steps, each of which has a chapter to itself.

The first step of the analysis is to divide the incoming text, whether spoken or written, into chunks that reflect natural breaks in the stream of text. A chunk is rarely smaller than a word, and while there is no specific limit on how many words in length it may be, it seems that most chunks are just a few words long, not often more than four or five. Chunking is a largely subliminal skill, and it is not open to negotiation. Reporting on chunking, the activity on which this study relies, could be a shaky foundation for an intellectual edifice, because it is open to influences from all kinds of hindsight, rationalisation, social awareness. If it goes beyond reporting a naive encounter with a text, matters of principle, consistency and explicability begin to assume a substantial presence. The chunking that is presented in the book began as the authors' individual reactions, which, when correlated led to a working principle that if in doubt we should insert a boundary rather than leave it out. By following this principle, we are less open to a charge of inconsistency; it would be very distracting to explain every quirk of our interpretations.

We begin by returning to the transcript which we examined word by word in Chapter 1 (Sample 1). It comes from the Lexis text (see Chapter 3) which was digitised before computers could handle both capital letters and small ones.

(1) a.   I HAVENT I DIDNT SEE ANYTHING BECAUSE IT WAS DURING THE NIGHT BUT IT WE WE CROSSED TO DENMARK IN THE MORNING

There are no explicit rules for placing the divisions; the ability to "chunk" a text is an intuitive skill; the divisions offered below are only one solution. These were argued in great detail in the Introduction so it is only necessary to present them briefly here:

(1) b.   I HAVENT
          I DIDNT * SEE ANYTHING
          BECAUSE

> IT WAS * DURING THE NIGHT
> BUT
> IT
> WE
> WE CROSSED * TO DENMARK
> IN THE MORNING

It was conceded in the detailed discussion that some speakers may prefer to have smaller chunks, and in that case may introduce additional boundaries where there are asterisks placed above. Any more atomised divisions will reduce the value of the chunking exercise, and there seems to be no motivation for further boundaries beyond the maximum proposed above. Access to the sound recording might suggest some changes, and it is stressed that the divisions are valid for this stretch of text only; no claim is intended that, for example, *in the morning* is never divided into *in* and *the morning*. The balance of all the features that tend to keep the text together and those that tend to divide it may fall in a different place on another occasion — though it would be surprising if *the* and *morning* were separated unless by a substantial pause or filled pause.

Those who incline towards larger chunks may prefer to have no division after *because*, and perhaps after *but*; our analysis tends to pick these items out because of our perception of their difference in function. The end result is not much affected by decisions of this kind, but the analysis is more explicit if they are separated at the first step.

In fast interactive conversation the chunks may be rather short; here is the first half of a turn, from the HKCSE text:

> (2) a. yea and then the other one is um er is the rice um like the i think

The speaker is clearly thinking out what to say while speaking, and needs to do several things at once — to control the timing, to retain the floor and to change direction when necessary, while all the time trying to make an effective increment to the shared knowledge. Our initial chunking of this extract is:

> (2) b. 1. yea
> 2. and then
> 3. the other one is
> 4. um er
> 5. is the rice
> 6. um
> 7. like
> 8. the
> 9. i think

Four of the provisional units that we have created are single words. The first unit has to be separate from the second because it is a response to the previous speaker, whereas line 2 continues a narrative. Line 6 is a filled pause to control the timing like line 4; line 7 is ostensibly a signal that an explanation is forthcoming, though it may also be supporting the function of line 6; line 8 is the beginning of a new statement but it does not get past the first word, being replaced by line 9, which is a return to the control of the interaction.

When a contribution from a speaker is "news-heavy" the chunks tend to be longer and there is less management of the interaction showing:

(3) a. the Estonian it was an article i read it was a famous Estonian tele- tel-evision i don't know reporter or something he went on strike on the hunger strike

This is the central part of a long turn in the ELFA text. The speaker is intent on presenting a complicated argument. We suggest the following chunking:

(3) b.
1. the Estonian
2. it was an article
3. i read
4. it was a famous Estonian tele-
5. television
6. i don't know
7. reporter
8. or something
9. he went on strike
10. on the hunger strike

Someone more inclined to make fewer boundaries might merge line 3 with line 2, but it would be difficult to merge any others because of their difference in function. Although line 5 and line 7 would go well together and make up "television reporter", they are split by line 6, which shows the speaker searching for a word. On the other hand even though several of the chunks have four or more words in them, there is little motivation for introducing additional boundaries.

In long written sentences the chunks largely follow the structural divisions of the grammar, as in example 4 from *The Independent* text:

(4) From now on, the Liberal Democrats have to present themselves as a party that wants power and knows what it wants to do if it gets it.

Our assignment of the provisional unit boundaries is:

1. From now on
2. the Liberal Democrats
3. have to present themselves
4. as a party
5. that wants power
6. and
7. knows
8. what it wants to do
9. if gets it

Each of the boundaries corresponds to an above-word grammatical boundary, but the correspondences between chunking and grammar is not entirely consistent. For example the chunk boundary at the end of line 4 is in the middle of a noun phrase, a minor grammatical break, while that at the end of line 2 is between subject and predicate, the principal division of the clause. Similarly the grammatical break between verb and object occurs within a chunk in line 3 but corresponds with a chunk boundary at the end of line 7.

The examples in this chapter show that, while there is a theoretical opportunity to place a boundary after each word, it is fairly easy to see a text as falling into small chunks, and to mark provisional boundaries. There is a great deal of uniformity in the way that different people place the boundaries, and a small amount of individual variation; however, the variation does not cut across boundaries of the kind presented here. Variations tend either to recognise some additional boundaries *within* those that we recognise, or just to *ignore* a few that are recognised in our analysis. Both kinds of variation are usually easy to assimilate in later stages of the analysis.

CHAPTER 6

Step 2: Types of chunks

This chapter presents the second step of our analysis, building on the output of Step 1 shown in the preceding chapter. The first step relied heavily on speaker intuition and a sense of 'naturalness' in chunking. From now on, the system becomes less intuitive and the categorisations of the chunks that were arrived at by the assignment of boundaries are done with reference to a system which is as rigorous as possible, while at the same time keeping in mind the inherent fuzziness of natural language.

With the chunk boundaries in place, then, we can turn our attention to the chunks themselves. They are of different kinds, and even though short and sometimes looking fragmentary, they seem to play different functional roles in the discourse. It is expedient to begin with the most fundamental distinction.

We distinguish two basic types of elements: those which are concerned with that which is being talked about (*it's a kind of mushroom; you have to use the language; in Denmark*), and those which are primarily concerned with managing the discourse (*yes; right; however; I suppose*). As shorthand symbols for these major categories we have chosen the letters M and O for their mnemonic value; the letter M almost inevitably suggests "message", and while this is convenient it should not be taken to imply that we adhere to the traditional view of a transferable message being encoded in text.

The fundamental difference between the major categories is intuitively clear to speakers and also reflected in many linguistic models, but hard to pin down in precise terms. Nevertheless, the two types can be characterised clearly enough to be recognisable by a speaker's intuition.[1]

The first kind of element takes forward the 'topic' that is being discussed; in some sense it constitutes 'that which is being said' in interactants' interpretation. To put it in another way, these elements increment the shared knowledge of the participants. Thus the unfolding discourse contributes to what interlocutors know as it moves along in small, processable chunks. These chunks, as separated by the PUBs, may not always seem successful or complete, but they contribute to the

---

1. We need to bear in mind that the intuition of speakers who might be doing this kind of analysis is heavily influenced by literacy and in most cases a good deal of linguistic education as well, which make their intuitions anything but truly 'naive'. This appears to be inescapable for practically anyone who can be used as an informant, and it is not possible to say whether it simplifies or complicates the task of identifying the units.

topical continuation rather than the process of making the discourse flow. This type of chunk we call *message-oriented element*, or M for short. This is the kind of element which is likely to appear in speakers' informal summaries of what was talked about or what somebody said. In interpreting spoken language speakers tend to abstract the content from not only things like replaced starts, repetitions and filled pauses, but many other clues that we make use of in constructing our ongoing interpretation of the discourse. In writing, filtering of this kind does not work in the same way because the writer does some of it on the readers' behalf, but the same processes are in operation, and the same categories result from both kinds of processing.

The other main type is the *organisation-oriented element* O. These elements help manage the utterance and the discourse. Participants need to negotiate meaning, and in the course of this negotiation it is necessary to manage turn-taking, changes of topic and the interrelations among chunks of contents and stretches of discourse. The need for constant management of the discourse is particularly obvious in the case of conversation. Conversation is co-operative, with speakers both competing with each other and helping each other. Conversation puts pressure on the interactants' real-time processing: turn-taking is often rapid and frequent, so that participants need to negotiate speaker and hearer roles constantly, and alternate in both roles. With simultaneous real-time utterance composing and interpreting, it follows that there is a lot to be managed, and we can therefore anticipate a number of elements that do not attempt to increment the topic directly.

The label 'message-oriented' is not entirely felicitous, as already pointed out above, since it has been associated with analyses where it is the only important, meaning-bearing part of the discourse, as if the other parts could be dismissed. In contrast, it could justifiably be argued that language elements with a primary purpose of expressing attitudinal stance or change of footing also carry a lot of meaning and therefore contribute to the 'message' that is shared between interactants. However, the M element as we want to use it is essentially oriented to incrementation of the topic, or shared knowledge, and is distinguishable from an element whose primary purpose is to manage the interactive aspect of the discourse. M elements realise something close to what Halliday calls the ideational metafunction of language (1985) and Sinclair (1982) the autonomous plane. The total meaning achieved in a conversation comprises much more than the M increments — involving paralinguistic and extralinguistic elements as well. The focus here is on what language can do in this whole rich experience, and at this stage we are concerned with what the main types of linguistic elements are that are needed for achieving these multiple ends within the time available.

What is important here is that the two main types of elements have fundamentally distinct and distinguishable functions which are not interchangeable; it is not so important whether similar utterances could on occasion be used for either purpose or whether in some instances we might not feel that an O element carries perhaps more referential meaning than usual. It is not essential either that there should never be any overlaps or unresolved cases. Many language units are multifunctional — which is no less than we expect from natural language. Natural language is not a sharp instrument with absolute or rigid boundaries, but is blurred at the edges. Even though the main category distinctions are clear and most units present no difficulty for analysis, the possibility of overlap and a certain fuzziness along the borders is to be expected.`

A further complication is added because our data is incomplete, and in some cases is like a shadow of the original event, which is lost for ever. We are not going to take the perfectionist path of trying to recreate or recapture as much of the detail as possible, but instead to take a more practically-oriented approach, essentially trying to make the best of what we have got. In this our task resembles much of real-life interaction in both the written and the spoken medium. Participants may be inexpert in the topics under discussion, or tired or uninterested; they may speak varieties of English with which some of the interlocutors are unfamiliar; there may be problems in the channel of communication, noise levels etc. Despite these distractions and obstacles, most interaction is reasonably successful at the levels of coherence, clarity and explicitness determined by the participants; as analysts we are working in an artificial environment, but our analysis would not necessarily improve in its relevance if we had access to far more precise and comprehensive data.

Let us look at some examples of M and O elements. For the first example we return to a snatch of conversation that was divided into PUBs in Step One; this fragment from the HKCSE text comprises one speaker's turn.

(1) a. 1. yea
2. and then
3. the other one is
4. um er
5. is the rice
6. um
7. like
8. the
9. I think
10. it's the
11. sort of
12. the roast beefs

The first two chunks do not seem to increment the content of the conversation. Line 1 starts the turn, and above all seems to mark the speaker change. Line 2 indicates that the speaker intends to move on to a new phase or the next topic to be tackled or a new element in the context. The first two chunks are thus best thought of as O elements.

Line 3 differs from the previous ones in that it seems to be stating something about the situation or topic (*the other one is*); it is not complete, but unmistakably part of a knowledge increment, therefore an M. The reason why line 3 remains incomplete is that it gets interrupted by line 4 (*um er*). The speaker is searching for an expression — in this case the speaker could actually be making up her mind as to what the next thing might be — and feels the need to say something to prevent another speaker from taking the floor (these are often dubbed "hesitations", one of the pejorative terms that we wish to avoid). Line 4 is thus an O element, while the following element (line 5, *is the rice*) makes a further contribution to what was begun in 3, and is an M — note the repeated *is*. Again, the next chunk (*um*) is a place holder and so is line 7 (*like*), so both are of the O type. But line 8 (*the*) begins something that is prima facie a knowledge increment, even though it is immediately interrupted by an attitudinal marker *I think* (line 9, an O). Line 10 resumes the incrementation begun in line 8 (*it's the*), which, after being interrupted by a hedging O element (*sort of*, line 11) is followed by a final content increment (*the roast beefs*). The whole example thus categorised reads like this:

(1) b. 1. yea   O
        2. and then   O
        3. the other one is M
        4. um er   O
        5. is the rice   M
        6. um   O
        7. like   O
        8. the   M
        9. I think   O
       10. it's the   M
       11. sort of   O
       12. the roast beefs   M

The next extract is from the Lexis corpus, entirely in upper case. The extract is part of a dialogue where one participant is telling a narrative. Since the transcript does not indicate pauses or speaker changes, and the original soundtrack is no longer available, the task of assigning unit categories is riskier than in contemporary recordings like the above example, which retain much more information from the original conversation. On the other hand, our ability to make sense of this transcript is testimony to the very skills on which this study is focussing.

(2) a. 1. IT WASNT VERY INTERESTING IN DENMARK
2. BECAUSE
3. FIRST OF ALL
4. IT WAS POURING WITH RAIN
5. OH DEAR
6. ABSOLUTELY POURING WITH RAIN
7. HA
8. YES
9. SO
10. I DIDNT REALLY ENJOY BEING ON THE BOAT

Here we have a similar alternation between M and O elements as above, even though the dialogue is rather different. To start by distinguishing the O elements, we can see that *because* in line 2 organises the interrelations of increments, which is one of the main functions of Os. So does the following element (*first of all*, line 3), even though these two are typically associated with a different 'level' or scope of discourse organisation; *because* is generally known as a clausal conjunction beginning a subordinate clause, while *first of all* is normally associated with the organisation of larger discourse relations, such as suprasentential units. At this stage of the analysis, however, such hierarchical distinctions are not relevant, since we are only concerned with the fundamental distinction between knowledge incrementing and discourse managing elements. In line 5, we encounter a chunk which is very likely an expression of empathy from an interlocutor (*oh dear*), thus managing the participants' interpersonal relations, and therefore an O. There seems to be a speaker change again at line 7 (*ha*), and again at line 8 (*yes*); even perhaps at line 9 (*so*), but it seems likely that lines 9 and 10 are said by the same person, the narrator, in which case so is also 8, and the interlocutor only manages lines 5 and 7. Lines 7, 8 and 9 are all elements of the O type: 7–8 expresses involvement in the narrative by both, and could be seen as minimal commentary. *So* introduces the next increment as a conclusion from the preceding narrative passage.

The M elements in extract 2 are longer than the O elements and much less fragmentary than in the previous example. They each increment the narrative with a further piece of information. The first line (*it wasn't very interesting in Denmark*) offers an evaluative comment on the speaker's experience in Denmark, and in line 4 (*it was pouring with rain*) we get part of the reason, as indicated by the intervening O elements. The reason is then repeated again (*absolutely pouring with rain*, line 6) after the expression of sympathy from the interlocutor. This is another M, although it mainly confirms the previous M with little alteration. Clearly, the self-repetition can be interpreted in interactive terms as well — the speaker is probably encouraged by the interlocutor's expression of involvement to repeat that which triggered the other participant's response the first time around. And in interactive terms this seems to have been good tactics, as is shown by the subsequent exchange of minimal responses. Increments may arise from interactive reasons, but how this comes about is outside our present concerns, since we are looking for kinds of linguistic elements, not motives for maintaining conversation. The final M (*I didn't really enjoy being on the boat*) clearly contributes to the shared knowledge again by providing an evaluative comment on the boat trip. Here is the analysis in all:

(2) b.
1. IT WASNT VERY INTERESTING IN DENMARK M
2. BECAUSE O
3. FIRST OF ALL O
4. IT WAS POURING WITH RAIN M
5. OH DEAR O
6. ABSOLUTELY POURING WITH RAIN M
7. HA O
8. YES O
9. SO O
10. I DIDNT REALLY ENJOY BEING ON THE BOAT M

For an entirely different example, let us turn to a very conventional piece of text. This is written language, from an editorial of a broadsheet newspaper (*The Independent*). The mode of presentation is completely monologic in the tradition of such texts, although the construction of meaning by means of this text is eventually interactive, involving the interpretive effort of the reader.

(3) a.
1. With that in mind,
2. he announced
3. two reviews,
4. one
5. to take a broad look
6. at policy,
7. the other
8. to look at
9. tax policy,
10. as well as
11. a number of
12. internal reviews
13. into the party's structure
14. and
15. communications.

The extract is conveniently delimited by its writer, so what we have is one sentence. The first chunk encapsulates what has already been said in the text and frames the rest. In this way, it serves as an organising, discourse managing element, and can be termed an O. With line 2, the writer adds to the knowledge we share about the situation reported in the text; thus we move on with the topic and have an M element. The third chunk continues by adding more to the shared pool of understanding (*two reviews*), until line 4 announces that what we are going to see next is the first of the reviews. Line 4 is thus an O element, and line 5 picks up the thread of the topic (*to take a broad look*). Line 6 builds on that. With line 7, a similar sequence begins again and the pattern repeats itself: first an O element (*the other*) telling us what is ahead, then two chunks moving on with the topic, until we reach another organiser in line 10 (*as well as*). This O element is again followed by increments to our shared understanding with the writer (lines 11–13), after which one more O element, *and* in line 14, announces the final incremental element in this sequence. The outcome of this breakdown is seen in (3b).

(3) b.
1. With that in mind,   O
2. he announced   M
3. two reviews,   M
4. one   O
5. to take a broad look   M
6. at policy,   M
7. the other   O
8. to look at   M
9. tax policy,   M
10. as well as   O
11. a number of   M
12. internal reviews   M
13. into the party's structure   M
14. and   O
15. communications.   M

Sometimes the distinction between the O and the M elements is less obvious than in the examples so far. One problem arises with minimal responses (*yes*), which can serve as informational elements (*yes* as an answer to a yes/no question) or as backchannelling (in the same way as *yea, mm, right* etc.). There is no inherent property in the items themselves which would determine the way in which they are used in a particular context. In cases like these, it is the context, specifically the immediately preceding discourse, which guides the interpretation of the unit. Consider the following extract from the HKCSE text:

(4) a. 1. ...A: okay okay
2. I know
3. I know
4. the
5. the long thin white one
6. right
7. B: yes
8. the long thin white one
9. A: uhuh
10. B: yea
11. and then
12. the other one is...

This is a short snippet which begins from the middle of A's turn, and ends in the middle of B's turn, but it is the exchange at the centre which is of interest, so the cut turns are there just to give a little more context. At the outset, in lines 1 to 6, A indicates that she recognises the kind of mushroom B is talking about (*the long thin white one*), using many interactive signals, and mentioning the target increment only once. When B takes up a turn (line 7), she first acknowledges A's recognition (*yes, the long thin white one*) in two chunks — the first element simply acknowledging the correctness of A's observation (*yes*), that is, confirming the sharedness of the knowledge accumulated at this stage.

This minimal response *yes* here also serves as a turn initiator for B, which she then follows up by repeating A's recent increment (*the long thin white one*). Now this repetition does not appear to bring anything new to the pool of shared knowledge, because this increment is already part of it. Rather, it confirms the sharedness of the understanding, and thus we can see it as serving an affiliative function. Could we then equally well categorise this as an O? As we already saw above in example 2, repeated increments can be interpersonally motivated, and can trigger further interpersonal exchanges, as other participants respond to the interpersonal aspect of the repetition. This happens in both example 2 and in 4, where the repetition is followed by an exchange of interpersonal elements in lines 9 and 10.

It is clear that repetitions do not bring much *new* to the shared knowledge, even though most of them seem to be partial repetitions, containing something new along with the repeated. It is nevertheless equally clear that the element in line 8 above operates as a topic increment, even though its novelty value is low; it is recognisably an element of the M type on the basis of the same criteria as the identical utterance it repeats. By being repeated, utterances gain particular rhetorical effects[2], and this is what is happening here. The interactive role is triggered off pre-

---

[2]. Scholars in the tradition of Conversation Analysis have discussed the role of repetition in the context of misunderstanding, misalignment or overlap — so if a speaker returns to his/her pre-

cisely on the basis of recognising the element as a repeated topic increment; the associations and connotations that this repetition brings about also depend on the recognition of its primary role as an M. Examples like this manifest the multifunctional potential of human language resources.

In the present analysis we must limit ourselves to a fairly narrow focus, to maintain the thread of the argument. We are aware that this may occasionally lead to downplaying the role of interaction, which is nevertheless not an indication of its lesser importance. We thus categorise the element in line 8 as M, keeping in mind the interactive potential of increments of this kind.

What we have, then, is the following analysis:

(4) b. 1. … A: okay okay   O
        2. I know   O
        3. I know   O
        4. the   M
        5. the long thin white one M
        6. right   O
        7. B: yes   O
        8. the long thin white one M
        9. A: uhuh   O
       10. B: yea   O
       11. and then   O
       12. the other one is   M

Sometimes the information we have is insufficient for resolving the categorisation of chunks, particularly if the chunk is very short. Some could realise either O or M, and the surrounding cotext in transcript form does not make it clear which function the chunk is fulfilling. Sometimes the original soundtrack can clarify, and in some cases the irresolvability results from a deliberate play with language, as in fiction. Let us look at another spoken extract, from the ELFA corpus, to illustrate a possible dual interpretation before moving on to take a look at how literary texts can play with this.

(5) a. 1. if you can't prove
        2. that
        3. you have the sufficient
        4. well

---

vious utterance by repeating it, he/she tries to draw attention to the overlapped sequence or to emphasise their position. CA is above all interested in analysing interaction, which is a different emphasis from ours, which puts priority on language as text.

5. that's what i believe
6. if you don't have
7. that
8. you have a sufficient

In this example, the problematic line is 5. The speaker interrupts herself in line 4, after starting to make a statement which she then apparently feels may be too categorical: she switches on to the interactive plane, distancing herself a little (*well*) from what she is saying. Line 5 (*that's what I believe*) can be seen as a continuance of this tack, providing an interactive comment, a hedge, before picking up the argument with a topic increment (*if you don't have*). We feel that this is the most natural interpretation of this chunk, given the cotext, but other analysts might want to see line 5 as an M element because it is a well articulated statement of the speaker's stance. It would in that case contribute to the development of the topic and its shared understanding among the speakers. Allowing for a dual interpretation in cases of this kind does not ruin the system of analysis, because it reflects the multifunctionality and fuzziness inherent in natural language. Our analysis of the extract is here as (5b).

(5) b. 1. if you can't prove   M
    2. that   O
    3. you have the sufficient   M
    4. well   O
    5. that's what i believe   O
    6. if you don't have   M
    7. that   O
    8. you have a sufficient   M

Among the often unclear ones are expressions like *sort of* and *kind of*. They may be either O elements or M elements, but it is hard to tell which in some cases. This is also true of certain other expressions. Let us now take a literary example and consider the following brief extract from Joyce's *Ulysses*.

(6) a. 1. I hope
    2. I'll never be
    3. like her
    4. a wonder
    5. she didnt want us
    6. to cover
    7. our faces

In this example, lines 1 (*I hope*) and 4 (*a wonder*) clearly satisfy the criteria for both M and O elements. *I hope* is a reporting clause, and contributes relevant knowledge, while it is also strongly attitudinal, expressing a stance. The interpretation definitely leans towards M by virtue of the position of the unit as a reporting clause in the present discourse. If *I hope* follows a clause for example in spoken interaction, it is clearly more attitudinal, and likely to be an O. *A wonder* resembles a unit of spoken discourse, consistent with the stream-of-consciousness technique used by the writer, which reports the protagonist's thoughts as if they were inner speech. Again, this chunk seems to contribute to the understanding being constructed between the writer and reader, and thus falls naturally into the M category. At the same time, it expresses a strong stance towards the topic of the discourse, which would motivate its interpretation as an O. It is not unlikely that the writer has used such ambiguity of interpretation deliberately. The analysis is then as follows:

(6) b. 1. I hope   M
       2. I'll never be   M
       3. like her   M
       4. a wonder   M
       5. she didn't want us M
       6. to cover   M
       7. our faces   M

The author also seems to be deliberately playing with multiple interpretability in the following extract (7), where we lack some crucial information relating to the element in line 4.

(7) a. 1. still
       2. I like that in him
       3. polite to old women
       4. like that
       5. and
       6. waiters
       7. and
       8. beggars
       9. too...

In line 4, *like that* can be thought of as relating to the preceding *old women*, in which case it would be an M element. However, it could also involve a more vague reference to the protagonist's musings over "him", marking a break in the train of thought before the list of other groups he was polite to. It can be seen as a similar move to *still* above, a potential turning point in the discourse — and in this interpretation it would be an O. We propose the following analysis:

(7) b. 1. still   O
     2. I like that in him   M
     3. polite to old women M
     4. like that   O
     5. and   O
     6. waiters   M
     7. and   O
     8. beggars   M
     9. too   O

The important point to remember here is that this is a literary representation of impromptu verbalised thought, and is no doubt constructed with attention to detail that belies the casual impression that it gives. Since there is no original sound to access, the writer is at liberty to keep us guessing about many features of expression, and there is in fact no obvious reason for trying to make decisions in cases like these. Our interpretation here marks O elements where a reasonable case can be made, to bring out the interactive flavour of the passage.

In sum, this chapter has begun to analyse the chunks separated by PUBs in step 1. We have presented here a primary distinction between elements which increment participants' shared experience (M) and elements which organise unfolding discourse (O). This distinction is not always unproblematic: some very short chunks are hard to classify reliably. More importantly, text in a social context typically assumes interactive meanings even when it increments shared experience. Despite this, most of the time it is not difficult to classify chunks into M and O elements. The distinction is fundamental, and typical instances are not easily confused. The distinction involves a binary choice, and the output of this step now bifurcates into further analyses of O (presented in Chapter 7) and M (Chapter 8) separately.

CHAPTER 7

Step 3: Types of organisational elements

The analytical model is taken onwards from the identification of the two main types introduced in the preceding chapter. We now need to characterise each type in more detail, and make further distinctions within each. First we discuss the O type in this chapter, and then continue with the M type in the next chapter. Dividing the steps in two chapters reflects the method of analysis: it is carefully staged, expecting the analyst to attend to one step at a time.

In the previous step the basic distinction between two types of provisional units was explained, and the O and M elements characterised. M elements are chunks which are interpreted as attempts, successful or not, to increment shared experience. O elements are the remainder, and they play a variety of roles in the conduct of an interaction and the interrelations of the M elements to each other.

This step and the one that follows, Step 4, are in parallel with each other, since they develop the O and M elements separately before bringing them together again. This step concerns only the O elements, which can be simply classified in the first instance, in another binary subdivision.

As hinted at the end of the first paragraph, one major task of the O elements is to attend to an ongoing interaction. Within this category of task, there are a lot of jobs to do — to intitiate the interaction and maintain it, to control the timing as much as possible, to structure the interaction by framing and focusing moves (Sinclair and Coulthard 1975), to manage a large repertoire of response strategies, to manoeuvre towards desirable outcomes, to "open up closings", to paraphrase Shegloff and Sacks' famous title (1973), and to close them. The speaker must be alert throughout the conversation, interpreting the interactive moves, guessing the shifting agenda of other participants and holding and yielding the floor as required. The verbal expressions of these objectives and tactics are labelled OI in this study, the I standing for *interactive*.

The other class of O elements contains elements that focus on the M segments rather than on the interaction. Shorn of the O elements, M segments are unordered with respect to each other beyond the primary sequencing of the text itself. They need to be placed in a multi-dimensional network of relationships; in Firth's terms (1968: 186) sequence must be replaced by *order*. Order can take many forms; in the broadest perspective of structural description there is a dimension which sets up hierarchies of organisation, in the discourse there is a dimension of interactivity, in sentence grammar there is a dimension of dependency, in cohesion/coherence there is a dimension of encapsulation and prospection (Sinclair 1993), while closer to the text there is a dimension which simply verbalises sequence, and several more. Without the O elements it might be difficult to understand a complex passage, even if all the relevant propositions were clearly verbalised in M units.

In this step we invoke the dimensions of textual coherence and interactivity, and divide the O elements into either OT, the text-oriented organisational units, or OI, the interactive-oriented organisational units. It is not always easy to apply this distinction, because the words and phrases which realise the O elements overlap a lot between OI and OT. Let us first look at simple cases. For example here is an extract from the Lexis text[1]:

(1) a. 1.   WE CROSSED IN THE MORNING
        2. B THE FRONTIER
        3.   YOU MEAN
        4. A YES YES
        5.   AND THEN
        6.   IT WASNT VERY INTERESTING IN DENMARK
        7.   BECAUSE
        8.   FIRST OF ALL
        9.   IT WAS POURING WITH RAIN
       10. B OH DEAR

Line 3 is the first O element, and it is requesting a clarification; hence it is primarily interactive and is assigned OI. Note that we posit a speaker change between lines 1 and 2, so our analysis does not coincide with the turntaking. The second speaker, Speaker B, we suggest, wishes to clarify what it was that they crossed, but first offers an M element, which would stand as an object to the verb *crossed* if they were in the same clause. Then B checks that his or her surmise is correct by using an interactive O element. Probably the speaker changes again, and it is now speaker A who utters line 4, which is a standard answer to a Yes/No question, and fulfils the expectation of line 3. It is an OI, adding nothing of substance to the record of shared experience. Speaker A continues with line 5, a fairly standard phrase for resuming a narrative; line 5, while an O, is an OT because it links the M element which follows to those which have gone before, in this case lines 1 and 2. This is the simplest kind of OT.

Line 6 is a straightforward M element, and line 7 is an OT because it expresses the textual relationship between line 6 and what follows (in this case line 9). Line 8 is also an OT because it prospects the future organisation of the text as a series of reasons in support of the opinion given in line 6. Line 10 we assume is said by speaker B and is an OI because it is understood as a sympathetic reaction to 9.

---

1. The second half of this example is the first half of example 2 of Step 2.

The distinction between OI and OT is not always clear-cut, and many O elements can have a partially interactive role while also organising the text; line 5, for example, may also be functioning as a place-holder while the speaker works out what to say next; arguably this could also be a feature of lines 7 and 8. Access to a sound or video recording might help to sort this out, but it turns out to be hardly necessary.

The analysis that this argument leads to is:

(1) b.
1.		WE CROSSED IN THE MORNING	M
2.	B	THE FRONTIER	M
3.		YOU MEAN	OI
4.	A	YES YES	OI
5.		AND THEN	OT
6.		IT WASNT VERY INTERESTING IN DENMARK	M
7.		BECAUSE	OT
8.		FIRST OF ALL	OT
9.		IT WAS POURING WITH RAIN	M
10.	B	OH DEAR	OI

Notice that line 6, which is the most substantial increment in the extract, is accompanied both before and after by OTs. Speaker A grabs back the floor with a possibly tetchy *Yes, yes* (meaning roughly 'it's obvious what we crossed') and cruises on until line 10. Speaker B seems to have trouble getting a word in edgeways.

In fact many of the details of the business of interaction do not survive the moment of utterance, and it is important to note that we do not here highlight the interactive nature of the conversation. In discourse analysis there would be an exchange boundary after line 1, for example, but it is also possible to see line 2 as a continuation of line 1 with a new speaker, a kind of collaborative completion of the kind pointed out in Conversation Analysis, e.g. Lerner (1991).

Returning to the list of functions of OT elements above, we see that line 5 is a verbalisation of sequence, line 7 relates lines 6 and 9 causally, and line 7 sets up a hierarchy of organisation, prospecting further causes to be mentioned.

OI elements are treated as textual units in the same way as the others. Whereas a discourse-analytical account of this passage might use the OI elements as major structural features, we concentrate on their role of enabling the M segments to be uttered effectively. The roles of OI and OT elements, seen from the point of view of M segments, is of first-level ordering (OT) and second-level ordering (OI). First-level ordering is direct and immediate and "inward"-looking in that its objective is to present the material of the text in a coherent and well-organised fashion, while second-level ordering looks "outward" to the circumstances in which the text will be presented, and aims for the efficient accomplishment of the utterance of the text.

It is important to appreciate that the distinction between OI and OT, and between them and M, is the end result of a process which is much more subtle than any labelling system can indicate. In the analyses presented here, the orderly succession of elements could suggest that the text is just a lump of "message", that has to be externalised, with the O elements negotiating its passage like tugs round an ocean liner. This is most unlikely to be the case; a variety of feedback systems operate during an interaction and unless it is a prepared statement the ongoing text is given its final shape at the last split second and in the process of its creation it undergoes modifications continuously.

Another example will perhaps clarify the distinction between OI and OT. This is from the ELFA text, with no change of speaker:

(2) a. 1. well
2. i think
3. in certain areas
4. you can
5. but
6. for example
7. in service
8. you can't

Line 1 is the start of a turn, and *well* is thoroughly established as a common item with which to start a turn. It serves to cushion the transition from one speaker to another, and if there is a gap between the prospections of the earlier speaker and the posture of the new one, *well* serves to bridge this gap, or to minimise its disruptive effect on the conversation. In this instance, the previous speaker has categorically said *you can't even get a job*, and although she immediately qualifies this with *officially*, it is a minor concession. Line 4 denies this statement, and *well* signals a lack of complete agreement.

Line 2 makes clear that what follows is a personal opinion, and there is a definite choice between OI and M. If it was an M, then it would be a main clause introducing lines 3 and 4 as reported clauses dependent on it. Since everything said is the speaker's thoughts in one way or another, there would have to be a reason for averring it in a position of prominence like this. As an OI, on the other hand, it is part of the apparatus that controls timing and presentation, and it just extends and slightly emphasises the cushioning effect of *well*.

In the present example the segments that follow line 2 do not give any grounds for proposing that line 2 should be classified as M; the shared uncertainty persists, so it is unlikely that the speaker is highlighting her definite personal position. The participants in this conversation are sharing their vague notions in the hope of verifying some of them. In line 5 the occurrence of *but* sets up a textual relationship of contrast, drawing attention to the polarisation of lines 3 and 4 on the one hand, and lines 7 and 8 on the other. The vagueness of *in certain areas* contrasted with the sharpness of *in service* adds to the uncertainty that pervades the passage.

The intonation and stress-pattern of the passage would probably clarify this assignment, but we are resolved not to consult it during the first analysis. The decision to classify line 2 as OI follows recognition by discourse analysts such as Aijmer (e.g. 2002) and Stenström (1994) that *I think* is normally found as a discourse particle rather than a reporting clause.

No 6 establishes a textual relation of exemplification, and as such is an OT. This is a medium-range pattern which organises the M elements from no 3 to line 8.

(2) b. 1. well   OI
        2. i think   OI
        3. in certain areas   M
        4. you can   M
        5. but   OT
        6. for example   OT
        7. in service   M
        8. you can't   M

In summary, this extract can be seen as a fairly typical beginning of what could be a lengthy turn. First the speaker secures the floor with two OI elements, giving herself quite a lot of room for manoeuvre. Then she makes her first, fairly tentative statement of an individual position, then sets up an organisation so that she can develop a more complex contribution. Everything except the statement is created by the O elements.

As we have said before, the demarcation lines of function here are not absolute, and while they are structuring the interaction the OI elements often express or imply attitudes or emotions that are part of the shared experience. Although the OI elements lose their structural relevance immediately, these aspects of their meaning are not transitory, and we have to find a way of adding them into the total record of shared experience; in LUG they form a set of notes in parallel with the analysed texts.

So our step of dividing segments into M and O is already cutting across the expectations of both conventional sentence analysis and discourse analysis. This present step marks out some of the O elements as OT, leaving a situation that can lead to their reunification with the Ms, as we shall see in Step 5.

Our analysis highlights a weakness of most existing grammars in the way in which they deal with OT elements. When a word or phrase like *and then, first of all* occurs it is classified as part of the nearest main clause, but that is essentially a convenience because these phrases have virtually no links with the clause to which they are assigned, and acquire names like "conjuncts" and "disjuncts", which sound almost disparaging. Some grammars call them "sentence adverbs", which at least shows that their constituency in a clause is a matter of convenience only — the clause is hosting them on behalf of the sentence. This situation arises because there is a constraint in most grammars that each sentence must be capable of division into a number of well-formed clauses, with nothing left over. There are only two possibilities; either each of these O elements has to be considered as a clause in its own right, or they must be merged, not very successfully, into the nearest main clause. Since OT units lack the propositional relationship that is considered a defining criterion of clause structure, the second alternative is generally considered superior. This problem is briefly set out in Chapter 1.

Linear Unit Grammar does not accept the constraint set out above. There is no need, at this stage anyway, to recognise the existence of clauses at all, let alone their internal composition. Let us examine an extract from the passage which contains the greatest density of O elements, HKCSE:

(3) A   yea   OI
    B   deep-fried pork chop   M
    A   yea   OI
    B   and then   OT
        with the oil   M
        butter   M
        um   OI

It is the fast interchange of speakers that accounts for the first two OI elements, and the third arises because the speaker has forgotten what to say, and is playing for time. The OT element is of the simplest kind, indicating narrative continuity. Clearly in this kind of text the organisation is handled by the O elements, and there is hardly a normal clause in sight.

The OI elements are associated particularly with interactive conversation, so, as pointed out above, we should expect few if any of them in written documents. But some literary effects are made by reversing the way in which the text is interpreted. The author inserts OI elements into a text that patently does not need them, and the reader conjures up an imaginary situation in which they would be relevant, required and informative. The "suspension of disbelief" convention that covers fiction is stretched at this point. Let us examine a short extract from the text written by James Joyce, the acknowledged master of such an effect.

(4) 1. a wonder   M
    2. she didnt want us   M
    3. to cover   M
    4. our faces   M

5.	but	OI
6.	she was	M
7.	a welleducated woman	M
8.	certainly	OI
9.	and	OI
10.	her gabby talk	M
11.	about Mr Riordan here	M
12.	and	OT
13.	Mr Riordan there	M

The word *but* usually indicates an OT, signalling the start of an M element which contrasts with what has gone before. But here, as in line 5, it lies between two expressions that are not really contrastive. A case could be made that someone who wanted women to cover their faces was not likely to be well-educated, but there is a way of accounting for this usage which does not require us to stretch our notions of contrast too much. We can interpret line 5 as an OI, as having more to do with the supposed interaction than with the rhetorical relations within the text. The word *but* can be used to re-set the parameters of the talk, as happens, for example, quite often when a speaker is regaining the floor after laughter or an interruption. People often say "Yes, but . . ." as a stock response just to establish that they have an independent stance, not necessarily that what they are about to say is in direct contrast with what has gone before. *But* is also used to resume an abandoned topic; Mazeland and Huiskes (2001) have investigated the resumptive functions of Dutch *Maar* and call this the "resuming *Maar*", i.e. the resuming 'but'.

The narrator has been saying highly critical things about 'her', she feels it necessary to redress the balance a bit, and introduces this positiveness with *but*. The contrast is not between the points she is making but in her quickly changing attitude to her subject. In no time she shifts back to bitchiness after *and*. Here a contrastive "but" would perhaps make her change of mood clearer.

Let us then consider the function of line 5 to be OI. The speaker is expressing rather loosely related reminiscences of "her", and it is appropriate to the style that the links remain loose, suggesting that the text is fairly impromptu. This impression is strengthened by line 8, which is also designated OI, and is an example of an item which is superfluous in the written mode; it suggests that the "speaker" is conducting an on-line review of what she is saying, and finds lines 6 and 7 to be worth confirming; there is a hint of concession about the usage. Line 9, like line 4, is usually classed as OT, but here the M elements are in such an obscure relationship to each other that there is no obvious way in which even the simple *and* relationship can link 6, 7 with 9 and what follows. The same word, however, at line 12, is a normal OT, with nos. 11 and 13 similarly phrased.

Joyce is writing here to give the impression of thoughts and images striking the speaker in real time, and being expressed with a minimum of organised connections, coherence or indeed clarity. We can see that it is intricately planned, with *but* and *and* being used in their interactive roles rather than their textual ones, and with frequent changes of posture.

To summarise the position with reference to organisational aspects of text, we first distinguish them from those which serve to augment shared experience. This was the job of Step 2, a binary choice. Step 3 involves taking a further binary choice, between those organisational elements which are principally focused on the interactive aspects of a communicative event, and those which are principally focused on the textual aspects.

It was demonstrated that during a conversation the interactive organisational elements provide the main structure, and that the familiar units of the grammar are fragmented and incompletely represented. In more formal spoken language events, the OI elements are less important, and in the written form of the language they are characteristically absent. The interactive organisation gives way to the textual organisation, and the OT elements carry the organisational load.

It is recognised that there are problems of identification and classification between OI and OT, and indeed OI and M, but that the choices have to be made because they profoundly affect the meaning. Some phrases, for example *I think*, can occur as conventional interactive elements, here labelled OI, or they can be firm expressions of the speaker's personal views, in which case they are M elements. Also, many words and phrases which are prime facie instances of textual organisation, such as *but* or even *and*, can be used as part of the tactics of interaction.

CHAPTER 8

Step 4: Types of increments to shared experience

In the previous chapter, we developed the analysis by looking more closely into the O elements, distinguishing subtypes among them. The M elements, which were the other main type, have not been elaborated yet. This chapter looks into the kinds of M elements that we need to distinguish in order to do justice to the kinds of incrementation that can be discerned in unfolding text. The point of departure here is again, as in Chapter 7, the output from the analytical step 2, described in Chapter 6.

On closer scrutiny, elements of the type we have called 'message oriented' are quite diverse within the limits of their general function. They all increment or attempt to increment the evolving topic. Not all increments are equally successful or complete: many remain incomplete, like "false starts", some are completed after brief interruptions or by a new speaker, and others mainly seem to add something to previous utterances. The wide variety of M elements is most obvious in spontaneous conversation, where speakers have very little chance of polishing their wordings before uttering them, and none at all afterwards. However, they can rephrase their first formulations, or modify, clarify, and expand what they uttered first.

Message oriented elements fall into several types on the basis of the kind of contribution they make to the progression of the shared topic matter. We distinguish seven types altogether, with another three possibilities of combination. The basic M element is called simply an M. An M element is a straightforward, mainly grammatical sequence which does not require anything else to complete it. Such elements often show normal clause structure, but this is not a requirement; sometimes a single nominal group is sufficient as a complete unit. In example 1, from the lexis text, we see a sequence of two Ms with normal clause structure separated by an OT, whereas in 2, from ELFA, the M element is a nominal structure.

(1) 1. I DIDNT REALLY ENJOY BEING ON THE BOAT   M
     2. BUT
     3. THE SCENERYS VERY FLAT   M

(2) 1. because
     2. the
     3. the Estonian government   M

    4. they made
    5. some kind of

In (2), the nominal structure in line 3 is not a 'complete' message in that it clearly anticipates something more to be said about the phrase — it is announcing a topic, and in the immediately following element we see it replaced by a coreferential pronoun (*they*) in the clause which develops the topic. Such placement of the topic ahead of the clause as it were, is a common phenomenon in speech, commonly known in formal grammars as 'left dislocation', but more positively termed as 'head' (McCarthy and Carter 1997), 'negotiating the referent' (Ford et al 2003), or 'negotiating topic' (Mauranen forthcoming b). At the level of local processing, we think a topic element of this kind is most naturally seen as an increment of the shared knowledge, in other words an M.

Although we expect to find M elements without normal clause structure mostly in conversations, they do appear in other types of discourse as well. Some written genres make plenty of use of nominal structure sequences, as illustrated here (3) from the Gazetteer text:

(3) 1. E. Malaysia   M
      2. (Borneo sts. of Sarawak and Sabah);
      3. cap. Kuala Lumpur;   M
      4. a. 334,110 km²;   M
      5. p. (est.1983) 14,744,000   M

Each of the M elements above constitute complete units of information in themselves, even though they are not clauses with finite verbs or other features commonly associated with 'whole' clauses, such as words spelt out completely.

Speech often gives the impression of being fragmented, especially if seen in transcription, because there are many elements which seem to begin something, but never continue far enough to seem to make a full contribution to the discourse. The speaker may get interrupted, change her mind, or hesitate about the formulation of the increment. Repetitions, especially repeated monosyllabic items (*the, the, the . . .*) which Biber et al.(1999) call "repeats", are generally thought to occur frequently in speech because speakers need processing time. These have been found at unit boundaries of different kinds - beginnings of units (Biber et al.1999), ends of units (Levelt 1989), and it has been suggested they might appear around formulaic sequences (Wray 2002). In all, pausing has been observed to occur at grammatical boundaries about half of the time (see Wray 2002), but this leaves much space for their occurrence at less predictable places.

Short elements which get abandoned when they have barely begun are in any case quite common in speech. We call these *message fragments* (MF); usually they are recognisably initiations of M elements, but sometimes they may also be so small that it is impossible to tell whether an incipient O or M element was meant. While it is somewhat arbitrary to label them all with an M, since OF units are theoretically possible, it would be even more arbitrary on the evidence of our sample transcripts to guess which might become M and which might become O. O elements tend to be shorter, less open in their construction and — if OI — they are often immediate reactions to real-time interactive movement; this suggests that they will be less likely to be planned or revised than M elements; hence it is likely that if a speaker adjusts his or her utterance by deploying an MF, it is an unfinished M rather than an unfinished O. Our data also contains several examples of MF elements that are longer than minimal, but not a single case of a longish but incomplete element which is recognisable as being of the O type. Since, further, MF elements play little part in the later stages of analysis, (see Chapter 9), ignoring the O/M distinction here will not noticeably distort the description.

Moreover, since these minor fragments are too small to make sense of reliably, their role in moving the conversation ahead is probably negligible and will not claim the interlocutors' attention for long. This is reflected in our model in subsuming them all under MF, and also in the way they are handled in later stages of the analysis.

Despite the inherent unlikelihood of "OF" elements being identified, we must keep an open mind until a lot more transcribed speech has been analysed in this way.

Typical examples of MF are seen in (4), from the lexis text, which shows the speaker beginning an M (line1), after which he replaces it with another initial element (line2), rendering the first start an MF. However, the second beginning is again replaced by another element — this time repeating the same start, so that the second start in turn becomes an MF. The third element then is an M, as if the speaker had finally decided how to go about this turn:

(4) 1. IT   MF
    2. WE   MF
    3. WE CROSSED TO DENMARK   M

The common explanation that repeats and pausing serve the purpose of 'buying time' for speakers is inadequate in making no provision for hearers. It is more likely that it benefits hearers as well as speakers, because both need spaces in processing. Field (2003) suggests that such 'dysfluencies' may assist non-native hearers, but it is unlikely that common linguistic phenomena would develop for non-natives' convenience if native speakers had no need for them (see Mauranen forthcoming a).

Not all interrupted elements are very brief; sometimes there is a meaningful beginning, which is left incomplete. Often the speaker makes a new start, replacing her fragment with a new element, as here in the ELFA text:

(5) 1. you have to use their   MF
     2. you have to use their language
     3. even in business
     4. it's   MF
     5. it's law now   M

This is the beginning of a turn, where the speaker begins to speak (line1), interrupts herself, and starts again. The second beginning (line 2) replaces the first and produces a completed M element. In lines 4–5 the speaker does a similar thing, although now interrupting herself early.

In conversations it is not unusual for an MF to result from an interlocutor's interruption which takes over the floor and makes a new beginning. We see this in (6), where two speakers are co-constructing an answer to a question asked a little earlier by one of them (B). A has not finished an answer before B chips in and starts to make his contribution:

(6) 1. A: you can't do   MF
     2. B: then   OT
     3. you can't even get a job   M

Sometimes an increment clearly has the feel of being an M element in its own right, but at the same time we interpret it as anticipating something more to follow. We call such an increment an *incomplete* M and use the symbol M– ("M dash") for it. It differs from an MF in that it is not interrupted in an obviously unfinished state, but nevertheless raises the expectation of another completing element. Thus, as distinct from an MF, which is a fragment and often merely gives a hint that it might have begun an M (or an O), a M– element manages to make a propositional contribution. To illustrate this, let us consider a part of the passage in example (2) above.

(2) b. 1. the Estonian government   M
        2. they made   M–
        3. some kind of   OI

Let us not worry about the continuation of the discourse at this point, but just focus on line 2. The element increments shared knowledge, but without making a full contribution before it is interrupted by an O element. Without considering whether the speaker manages to continue this element, we notice that there is a strong prospection of a continuation. As the intervening element is an O and not a replacement nor an M element with a new beginning, this is not an abandoned fragment. An M– thus leaves no doubt that it is a message-like element, and it clearly contributes to the shared knowledge, but at the same time it raises a strong expectation that it will be completed by something else.

The element which completes an M– is given the symbol +M ("Plus M") for *completion of M*. A +M is thus defined as an element which supplies appropriate completion material to an M–. They normally appear in pairs, as seen in (7). The first pair in lines 2 and 3 is immediately adjacent, and in the second pair in lines 5 and 7 only a minimal MF intervenes, which does not disrupt the continuity between the members of the pair. We have not found any examples in our material of an M– which is not paired with a +M shortly after, but there is no good reason why this should not occur in the vagaries of conversation; prospection is not always successful, and we presume that the M– simply remains incomplete.

(7) 1. A: erm   OI
    2. if you have a direct contact   M–
    3. with the people   +M
    4. and   OT
    5. you don't have   M–
    6. s-   MF
    7. efficient Estonian   +M

A conversational topic increment has a short lifespan; if the same topic appears later, after another turn or so, it must be regarded as a new start, or a re-start of the topic. Thus if a topic reappears after a while it is not a completion of an earlier mention even if the element was left incomplete the first time.

Speakers in conversation may jointly construct M– +M pairs, as in (8). In fact, such 'collaborative completion' where interlocutors complete each other's utterances is quite common, as is well known from discourse and conversation analytical work (see, e.g. Selting and Couper-Kuhlen 2001).

(8) 1. B: I'm not sure   OI
    2. it must be   M–
    3. A: kind of mushroom   +M

In written language we do not expect to find MF units, because even if the writer changed his or her mind or modified the text after a first draft, these have been deleted from the final product. In contrast, there are no barriers to M– and +M pairs appearing in written text, and in fact we see them frequently (example 9).

(9) 1. Sounding nice   M–
    2. is no longer enough,   +M
    3. he argued.   M

There is one remaining type of interrupted element which needs to be recognised as a separate kind. This is a minor 'bump' in a speaker's turn, which leaves an element incomplete but does not abandon it by replacing it with a new start:

(10) 1. it was a famous Estonian tele-   MA
     2. television   +M–
     3. i don't know   OI
     4. reporter   +M
     5. or something   OI

Here it is clear that the speaker, after a self-interruption (line 2) repeats only the individual item which was left incomplete and continues as if the interruption had not occurred, that is, the incrementation to the discourse is jointly achieved by lines 1 and 2, with the additional syllable of the first stab at *television*. An M which is thus interrupted and modified in progress is called *message adjustment* (MA). An MA prospects a completion in that it characteristically provides a nearly complete increment. In this it can be likened to an M– but contrasts with an MF, which makes no prospection. Completions to MA elements are marked +M in line with other completions; for the M element that follows an MF we keep the symbol M because no relationship of prospection — fulfilment is involved.

Looking at the way the turn continues in this case, the interruption in the first line may reflect processing problems ahead, because the speaker soon indicates (line 3) her difficulties in finding an expression for the status of the 'television person'.

This example also shows a combination element +M– (line2), which is at the same time a completion of the element above and itself anticipating a continuation. The prospected completion does not follow immediately, because the speaker shifts to an OI comment, but immediately after that the continuation appears. Combinations are discussed briefly towards the end of this chapter.

Just as we interpret some elements as strongly anticipating something else to follow, there are others which do not make a prospection (an example would be a plain M) and there are some which are not anticipated at all. Elements in this last category follow another element, and provide an addition or specification but do not start anything new. These are distinct from +M in that they do not fulfil a previous prospection; instead they add something to an M which is complete already (see chapters 1 and 11). In terms of position, they are the mirror image of M– elements. We call such elements *message supplements*, or MS for short. They are often adjuncts of time or place (as in 11), or specifying elements of a similar kind (12). An M may be followed by several of these (13).

(11) 1. WE CROSSED TO DENMARK   M
     2. IN THE MORNING   MS
     3. I REMEMBER   OI
     4. FROM HAMBURG TO GEDSER   MS

In 11, the OI element (line 3) is inserted between the two MSs, but does not interfere with the continuity of the discourse — it is short and within one speaker's turn. Below, the MS follows the M immediately (12).

(12) 1. you have to use their   MF
     2. you have to use their language M
     3. even in business   MS

In written text, MS elements are also used, and writers just like speakers can use a number of them following one M, as in this extract from Joyce (13), where the many MSs may seek to produce the illusion of a person's internal monologue.

(13) 1. still   OI
     2. I like that in him   M
     3. polite to old women   MS
     4. like that   MS
     5. and   OT
     6. waiters   MS
     7. and   OT
     8. beggars   MS
     9. too...   OT

We also find MS elements of a more unusual kind in specific genres, as in this gazetteer entry (14), which has its own conventions. The MS elements consist of details which follow the M elements in a regular manner:

(14) 1. Malaysia,   M
     2. Federation of,   MS
     3. indep.federation   M
     4. (1963),   MS

It is quite common in spoken discourse to find elements which repeat or slightly reformulate an earlier one. More precisely, this involves reworking an element which has already occurred in the immediately preceding context. We call these elements MR (*message revision*). A typical case is (15), from the lexis text, where A is telling a narrative. A gives a conventional background description, and after a sympathetic interactive insertion from B repeats the element with a small expansion, in this case intensification.

(15) 1. A: IT WAS POURING WITH RAIN   M
     2. B: OH DEAR   OI
     3. A: ABSOLUTELY POURING WITH RAIN   MR

The modification above is very slight, and sometimes there is none, as in (16), from the HKCSE text. We already discussed the interactive potential of repetition in dialogue above in Chapter 6. Here the verbatim repetition seems to play an affiliative role, and because A is a non-native speaker and B a native speaker of English we can also surmise that B's repetition may confirm A's formulation.

(16) 1. A: ... I know   OI
     2. the   MF
     3. the long thin white one M
     4. right   OI
     5. B: yes   OI
     6. the long thin white one MR

The different types of M elements have now been distinguished. It is not necessary for us to establish further categories at this level, and although subdivisions which take the analysis to subtler details are naturally possible, needlessly proliferating categories is a danger we want to avoid. Nevertheless, we need to point out that while we stay at the present level of analysis, the different M element types can also combine with each other to an extent, as was already seen in connection with example (10) above.

It is relatively common for +M and M– to combine into a single element. We see this in (17), from *The Independent* text. In line 3, the M element continues what was begun in the first line, before the O element intervenes, but at the same time it makes a strong prediction that it will be followed by at least one more element. The sequence fulfilling this prediction starts with the O element in line 4. The M– and +M in lines 5 and 6 pair up as a complete unit, and the last element in this extract tops the message up with a supplementary specification.

(17) 1. Mr Kennedy   M–
     2. now   OT
     3. declares   +M–
     4. that   OT
     5. it must be   M–
     6. bold   +M
     7. in its thinking MS

The combination element +M– can also form sequences of more than one such elements even in written text. Example (18), from the Joyce text, is perhaps not a characteristic everyday text, but it illustrates the potential for writing of this kind in simulating the protagonist's train of thought, with a hint of imaginary dialogue in it:

(18) 1. I hope   M–
      2. I'll never be   +M–
      3. like her   +M
      4. a wonder   M–
      5. she didnt want us +M–
      6. to cover   +M–
      7. our faces   +M

In addition to the fairly common combinatory element +M–, there is one case in our data where +M combines with an MF. This sole instance (19), from the ELFA text, is from a situation where English is spoken as a lingua franca, and is thus not anyone's native language. The extract below is longish, because the context makes it easier to follow what is going on.

(19) 1. A: ... if you can't prove M–
      2. that   OT
      3. you have the sufficient   +MF
      4. well   OI
      5. that's what i believe   OI
      6. if you don't have   MF
      7. that   OT
      8. you have a sufficient   M–
      9. er   OI
      10. knowledge   +M–
      11. B: yeah   OI
      12. A: of Estonian   +M

The speaker in 19 seems to lose track of the phrasing a little. The sidetrack sequence in lines 4–5, which is a disclaimer or hedge, seems to throw the speaker slightly off balance, so what we get is a fresh start on the bigger point in line 6, but even that proceeds somewhat uneasily. This extract was not really possible to analyse with certainty without consulting the soundtrack and so is one of the rare cases where we returned to the original recording: in line 6, *have* gets focal stress, and *that* which follows in line 7 is unstressed. In line 8 we have a similar element to line 3 resuming the topic, but unlike the earlier attempt, this time the M element is followed by a complementing element (line 10), which continues (line 12) after the interlocutor's supportive comment in line 11.

In addition to the two combination elements, others are possible, and our data includes one more kind, which can be seen in example (21) below: an MS–. The combinations are thus possibilities of bridging two elements which for one reason or another are separated, but which have a relationship of prospection and its fulfilment.

Sometimes formally identical units have a different status assigned to them. This is to be expected, because natural language elements participate in meaning-creation in different ways depending on their context. Any context-sensitive model will have to account for this, and since we maintain linearity as a major principle in our model, relative position is very important, as we would expect it to be in ordinary language processing. So for example *if*-clauses have been in most cases analysed as M– elements, as for instance in (20). Often these elements do, as here, occur in contexts where they anticipate another clause to follow.

(20)
1. A: erm — OI
2. if you have a direct contact — M–
3. with the people — +M
4. and — OT
5. you don't have — M–
6. s– — MF
7. efficient Estonian — +M
8. then — OT
9. you can't get it — M

The turn-initial *if*-clause is a classic example of the *if — then* relationship in argumentation: the *if*-clause (line 2) indicating a condition comes first. As here, it may be followed by further specifications (lines 3–7), which function as additional premises in the relationship. After this follows an OT (line 8) indicating that the status of the element to follow in the argument is the predicted consequence, and finally (line 9) comes the consequence itself. This prospection made by the initial *if*-clause thus spans several elements. It constitutes a structured whole at the discourse level, which we can posit as a basic-level discourse structure (see Mauranen forthcoming a). The longer-span structuring is achieved by prospective elements (the *if*-clause) together with the OT elements signalling the organisation of the structure (*and* in line 4 and *then* in line 8). It is quite likely that the familiar schema of the *if — then* relationship also efficiently supports the perception of this organisation.

An *if*-clause does not always present a condition predicting a consequence. In the extracts sampled for the present analysis, an *if*-clause also appeared in utterance final position, or more precisely sentence-final in this case, which comes from a written text, *The Independent*. The whole sentence is quoted below (21).

(21)
1. From now on, — M–
2. the Liberal Democrats — +M–
3. have to present themselves — +M
4. as a party — +M
5. that wants power — MS

6. and	OT
7. knows	MS–
8. what it wants to do	+M
9. if it gets it.	MS

Clearly here the *if*-clause (lines 9 and 10) is not predictive of anything, nor does it present a condition paired with its logical consequence. The *if*-clause presents a hypothetical situation, but there is no clause indicating a consequence that would ensue if the hypothetical condition was realized: in case the *if*-clause situation were fulfilled (i.e. the Liberal Democrats got power), it would not follow that they would want to do something in particular, let alone that they would know what to do; they might or might not, but it would not necessarily be a consequence of the situation. The *if*-clause specifies the circumstances in which such behaviour (wanting to do something) is relevant, but not a condition for a consequence. What the *if*-clause thus does is add a specification to the preceding element pair (lines 7–8). Consequently it is an MS in the present descriptive system.

As we have seen in this chapter, a closer look into M elements discloses several subtypes. We have performed a more fine-grained subcategorisation of M elements than we did with the O elements. This is partly a response to the dominance of Ms in written text and our desire to integrate the analysis of writing and speaking in one model. We have nevertheless kept the M subcategories to the minimum while accounting for all of the data. Since our data comes from a wide range of text types, it is likely that the most important M categories are included in the system, even though it is possible that the need may arise for distinguishing new types. Seven subcategories may seem a lot, but there is more order in the chaos than perhaps first meets the eye: when we give a skeleton summary of the categories in the analytical system in Chapter 12 (section 'Summary of Linear Unit Grammar'), we show that all the subtypes of M reflect a set of binary choices, just as the present system of analysis does as a whole.

CHAPTER 9

Step 5: Synthesis

This chapter finishes the presentation of the analytical system — it draws together the results from the preceding four steps, thus rounding off the model presented. At the same time, it paves the way forward, and provides an interface with LUG and other analyses, showing that although our approach is unconventional, it is not incompatible with other traditions.

We now come to the final stage, and recombine the elements that we have been classifying so that they are available for further descriptive analysis, either using an existing grammar or one that will be suggested later in this book (Chapter 11), or for a range of other applications.

We go through a set of operations which build on the outcome of the analysis performed in the four steps above. These operations help to bring about a formulation of the text which is conventional enough to serve as input to further grammatical analysis.

There are eight operations in all, most relatively simple and straightforward, some more complex and open to further negotiation. We illustrate each of these with a brief extract from the data, and after the individual operations show how they come together in a new synthesis.

We begin the operations from the O elements, of which there are fewer than Ms, and work our way through all elements which could be removed, modified or combined while retaining the meaning of the original discourse as fully as possible.

First, the elements classified as OI are removed from the linear stream, and are put aside for the moment for a later stage in the recombination process. That is, they are turned into notes and comments on aspects of the interaction which contribute to the incremental meaning. These accompany the linear text. For example:

(1) a. 1. if i'm a Russian   I M
        2. living in Estonia   MS
        3. like   OI
        4. (if) i don't speak Estonian   M–
        5. can i legally open a shop +M
        6. or   OT
        7. er   OI
        8. work at this shop   +M

Line 3 is OI, providing an adjustment to make a coherent movement from line 2 to line 4. It is necessary to indicate that line 4 fits into the argument by reminding the listeners that the main topic concerns the learning of Estonian, so there is a hint of OT about line 3 that must be borne in mind later in this step; on the other hand it is an interpolation in the way in which the structure is developing, the kind of ad hoc addition that does not deflect the main argument. Line 7 is also OI, and is a "filled pause", where the speaker wishes to keep the floor while preparing to phrase the next point. If our judgement is that it is simply a matter of timing in the interaction, there is no need to retain this item at all; it did its job at the time of utterance, but it has no long-term meaning to contribute.

We can then remove line 3 and line 7, leaving the passage:

(1) b. 1. if i'm a Russian   +M–
        2. living in Estonia   MS
        3.
        4. (if) i don't speak Estonian   M–
        5. can i legally open a shop   +M
        6. or   OT
        7.
        8. work at this shop   +M

We also make a note that line 4 is isolated and needs to be integrated into the final form of the unit. The remainder consists of the M elements and the OT elements in their original sequence. We return to the final form of this example later.

The second operation is concerned with M elements, beginning with message fragments. We now remove the MF elements, for example:

(2) a. 1. the   MF
        2. I   MF
        3. I'm not sure   OI
        4. it must be   M–
        5. kind of mushroom   +M
        6. it's a kind of mushroom   MR
        7. the Japanese mushroom   MR

Here the speaker has second thoughts about line 1 and line 2, and these can just be removed. However, we need to pay attention to the possibility that some reconsidered starts have meaning beyond the moment of utterance, and should lead to accompanying notes. As pointed out above, we need to make notes on any operations that affect aspects of meaning which might be important to retain. The notes will be considered for the final operations, and utilised for adjustments in the outcome of this phase. The kinds of notes worth keeping of course depend on the purpose of the analysis at hand.

As the next operation, we remove the conversational bumps caused by MA elements. The MA elements are made up of parts which contribute to the incremental meaning, and something which is fragmentary or repeated. The former remain for any further analysis, but the latter will normally be deleted on account of being unnecessary. In each of the cases we had in our data the MA included something that was repeated later. Let us consider example (3a).

(3) a. 1. I think   OI
        2. it's the   MA
        3. sort of   OI
        4. the roast beefs +M

Lines 1 and 3 are OI elements; the OI in line 1 is attitudinal, and indicates the speaker is not quite sure about the identity of the next item she is talking about. It is a good idea to make a note about this element for later use. Line 3 is an OI whose meaning is only relevant to the management of the interaction in its original context, and we can remove it. As a result, we now have (3b).

(3) b. 1.
        2. it's the   MA
        3.
        4. the roast beefs +M

We are left with two different M elements, an MA which makes a beginning but is left incomplete, prospecting a continuation, and a +M which provides the completion. We can now put these together, with the simple removal of the superfluous repetition of *the*. And so we get

it's the roast beefs

After this, we put together pairs of M- and +M when they are next to each other; this brings together M units which were separated by a PUB, or perhaps by an intervening OI. In our example (2) we merge line 4 and line 5, and as we will also have deleted the OI at line 3, this gives us

it must be kind of mushroom

The example now reads:

(2) b. 1. it must be * kind of mushroom   M
        2. it's a kind of mushroom   MR
        3. the Japanese mushroom   MR

We have noted the absence of an article after *be*, for later attention.

Next we add MS elements to the nearest previous M, as in the following example, which is now from a written text:

(4)   1. I like that in him   M
      2. polite to old women   MS
      3. like that   MS

The PUBs can be removed, giving one continuous M unit; however, the boundaries may have concealed some lack of explicit coherence, which becomes obvious when the text is reassembled; in the case of (4) our judgement is that the word *that* in line 1 prospects line 2 and line 3, and it pre-assesses line 2 and line 3 as examples of what the "I"-person likes. This is conveyed by an adjustment in the punctuation (4b), which gives the text a more conventional form.

(4)   b. I like that in him, | polite to old women | like that

A vertical line is placed at the start of MS units to allow recall of the MS unit at a later stage; often, but not always, these may be suitable places for the insertion of a comma in writing — in (4b) the first comma is mandatory but there is no need for a second.

These three adjustments of subcategories of M begin to give us some longish stretches of M, interspersed with OT elements to indicate the way in which the M units are organised with respect to each other.

The remaining element is MR, which repeats or reformulates an earlier element. In this case, the recombination operation is to eliminate the elements which make much the same contribution to the shared knowledge. Thus only one M must appear in the final text. The exact formulation of this M is a matter of judgement; often the last formulation is what the speaker is most happy with — but sometimes an earlier one, or even a blend of more than one formulation is superior. The final formulation must be prioritised because by moving on the speaker clearly indicates that the formulation is good enough for its purpose. But for the participants in the speech situation, something may remain from earlier formulations that contributes to the shared understanding. There are no rules for a definitive interpretation as yet, and occasionally the merging of MR elements could lead to a note being appended to the text to explain the effect of the repetition or rephrasing.

We return to example (2) to illustrate alternative possibilities in merging MR elements into one.

(2)   c.   1. it must be * kind of mushroom   M
           2. it's a kind of mushroom   MR
           3. the Japanese mushroom   MR

These three elements should be merged to give just one, and there are several possible solutions; perhaps the simplest is:

(2) d.   it must be a kind of Japanese mushroom

But if you interpret it so that *a kind of mushroom* is a preliminary formulation of *a Japanese mushroom*, then one solution is:

(2) e.   it must be a Japanese mushroom

Another interpretation would be to add a change of posture between lines 2 and 3.

(2) f.   It must be a kind of mushroom — a Japanese mushroom

There is a speaker change after each of the original segments — lines 4, 5 and 6 in (2a) — so it is to be expected that they do not fit together precisely. The third version of the merged M element, (2f), reflects the emergence of a precise concept from the exchanges. Of the originals, *it must be* is preferred to *it's*, but the phrasing then follows (2c2), and then (2c3) is added as a new posture, with the indefinite article preferred to the definite article.

Now we have covered all O and M elements. What remains are some further adjustments to finalise the recombination process. Consider the following example:

(5) a.   1. WE CROSSED TO DENMARK   M
          2. IN THE MORNING   MS
          3. I REMEMBER   OI
          4. FROM HAMBURG TO GEDSER   MS
          5. I THINK   OI
          6. A PLACE CALLED GEDSER   MR

We omit the OI elements (lines 3 and 5) and add the MS in line 2 to the M in line 1. Then we have to resolve a single coherent segment out of lines 4 and 6. The easiest merging of these two is: *from Hamburg to a place called Gedser*, giving us a single M unit:

(5) b.   WE CROSSED TO DENMARK | IN THE MORNING, | FROM HAMBURG TO A PLACE CALLED GEDSER

Then we must consider which of the information we have suppressed is germane to the incrementation of shared understanding; if it is, it will have to be retained somehow. For line 3, which is largely in place to control the real-time interaction, the comma is a reasonable expression. The omission of line 5 removes a certain hesitancy which the speaker showed in recalling the place-name Gedser. This is reasonably retained in the distancing effect of *a place called*, and does not need any further attention.

After these adjustments, most texts will be looking fairly like well-formed, conventional written prose; but there may still be some abrupt transitions, missing links or the like. The analyst makes the minimum adjustment to the text by way of changing the sequence or making a relationship more explicit. There has to be justification for each adjustment, however minimal — for example a change in posture which would be unacceptable within an utterance of a single speaker needs to be supported by a word like *but* when indications of speaker change have been removed.

For example, we can now finish (1) by writing out (1b) as a single unit, (1c)

(1) c. if i'm a Russian | living in Estonia* i don't speak Estonian can i legally open a shop or work at this shop

The asterisk is to remind us that the following phrase has to be integrated into a version of the text which is not coping with real-time considerations. Perhaps the minimum adjustment in this case is to replace the asterisk by *and*. With some tidying up of the orthography and punctuation the unit now reads:

(1) d. If I'm a Russian | living in Estonia, <u>and</u> I don't speak Estonian, | can I legally open a shop <u>or</u> work at this shop?

The OT unit *or* is underlined here to remind us that this aspect of the segmentation remains. A vertical line is placed at the MM boundaries as a reminder of analysis that has been established here. Note that the added *and* would be classified as OT if it had actually occurred.

To summarise: the operations that make up Step 5 are various omissions, concatenations and adjustments. Each one distorts the original text, and some parts of that distortion may be interpreted as aspects of meaning that should not be lost. In such cases it is necessary to make notes, some of which are then used to justify adjustments of the text at operation 6 below.

1. Remove OI elements
2. Remove MF elements
3. Reconcile MA with the following +M
4. Reconcile M– to the following +M
5. Add MS elements with the preceding M
6. Merge MR elements with the M elements of which they are reformulations
7. Adjust text to take account of notes
8. Make any further adjustments of text towards written norms.

Where an analytical boundary is obscured by removal of intervening material or in operation 5, a vertical line is placed in the text as a reminder that the boundary is available for later use in description if necessary.

In the case of ordinary written text, most of the adjustments described here do not arise. OI elements would only appear if the text was simulating real-time interaction. Any MF would be deleted by the writer. We would expect the text to be largely a sequence of OT and the other M elements. Boundaries introduced at Step 1 of the chunking would largely be deleted during operations 3 to 5.

There should be very few MR elements in written text and these might be reformulations for rhetorical effect — the analyst should adopt a specific policy for these depending on the object of the analysis:

(a) if the object was, broadly speaking, information extraction, then the MR elements could be merged in Step 6, with notes added to explain the deletions;
(b) if the object was the exploration of style, e.g. literary or oratorical devices, then the merging of MR elements would tend to obscure features of repetition or parallelism, and so this step would be omitted.

If all text was tidy and conventional, observing written language norms, then the descriptive apparatus detailed here would not be worth carrying out. We include samples of written text, not to show how revelatory our analysis is with this kind of text, but to show that the same set of categories and descriptive methods will accept all kinds of text and produce output in a standard format.

Here is an example of ordinary written text:

(6) a.
1. to look at	M–
2. tax policy	+M
3. as well as	OT
4. a number of	M–
5. internal reviews	+M
6. into the party's structure	MS
7. and	OT
8. communications	MS

The third operation reconciles lines 1 and 2, and also lines 4 and 5. The fourth operation adds line 6 and line 8 to line 5, and we are more or less back where we started. The only traces of the analysis are the classifying of line 3 and line 7 as OT, and in (6b) these are underlined to make the point that there has been some segmentation.

(6) b.   to look at tax policy <u>as well as</u> a number of internal reviews | into the party's structure <u>and</u> | communications.

There are easier ways of reaching this result, but in considering the analysis that works on the output of Linear Unit Grammar, the ability to describe all texts with the same apparatus is a valuable move in regimentation.

Returning to the conversation transcripts, where Linear Unit Grammar does claim to make a contribution to understanding as well as regimentation, we have to accept less than total coherence on some occasions. Ultimately in spoken interaction coherence remains unexamined; only incoherence requires explanation, and some levels of incoherence can be tolerated. Whatever passes without challenge among participants in conversational interaction is assumed to be sufficiently coherent for the time being. As the discourse is co-constructed between the participants, elements may be cast aside because the conversation takes a new turn and they are no longer perceived as relevant, or because they are judged to be unimportant at the outset. Such elements can simply be neglected, overlooked, or ignored, and unless a later twist of the conversation brings them back into focus, they may remain forever obscure.

This is a major difference between the written and spoken mediums; anything written is assumed to be perfectly coherent in every detail, and lives and fortunes depend on this convention being observed; there are gradations within the convention, with legal pronouncements being formulated with great care, and scribbled notes and e-mails following less rigid rules of interpretation. While there are similar gradations in speech, only read-out written statements need follow the norms of written language.

Another area of difference is that people do not always articulate exactly what they would like to say; most people find it hard to formulate novel or abstract thoughts even if they think these are important; what is regarded as less important to formulate precisely tends to get even less attention — like turns in idle chat. Speakers using a foreign language often need to struggle more with expression, and their speech tends to have many reconsiderations, reformulations and pauses; they also deviate more from standard grammar and conventional expressions.

In addition to inherent differences in the production mode, transcriptions of ordinary talk are notoriously indeterminate in places, and each time an extract is transcribed differences arise. These are usually in minor areas but not always.

With these cautions in mind, we end this section with a longer example; of all the sample texts that we studied, this passage is the most difficult to make satisfactorily coherent. It is one complete turn by an expert, but non-native, speaker of English.

(7) a. 1. and   OT
        2. i mean   OI
        3. it's funny thing   M
        4. because   OT
        5. the   MF
        6. the Estonian   MF
        7. it was an article M

8.	i read	MS
9.	it was a famous Estonian tele–	MA
10.	television	+M–
11.	i don't know	OI
12.	reporter	+M
13.	or something	OI
14.	he went on strike	M
15.	on the hunger strike	MR
16.	because	OT
17.	er	OI
18.	the	MF
19.	the Estonian government	M
20.	they made	M–
21.	some kind of	OI
22.	simplifying	+M–
23.	towards the citizenship law	+M
24.	for the Russians	MS
25.	so	OT
26.	he went to the hunger strike	M
27.	because of	OT
28.	the(ir) thinking	M
29.	that	OT
30.	it's	MF
31.	it's unfair	M

The transcription contains just one doubtful syllable, in line 28, and in this case we returned to the sound recording, but without much illumination; the diphthong is elongated and the intended word could be *the* or *their*. A somewhat archaic construction in English, "because of their thinking that…." is just a possiblity, but at present we prefer it to remain ambiguous at *the(ir)*.

The first operation is to remove the OI elements, paying attention to any meaning which they supply and which should be retained. In the case of line 2, *I mean*, this seems to be relevant only to the interaction — confirming that the speaker keeps the floor and is continuing from a previous position, restating it in different terms.

Before continuing to remove the OI elements, we discuss line 3 in a little detail. It proved a difficult line to classify because it might contribute in more than one way to the meaning and organisation of the passage. It seems to be at least in part functioning as a place-holder, keeping the floor as the speaker reorients to a new approach to the topic that starts in line 7. If that were its only or main function it should be classified OI; implicit in this decision is the judgement that no account needs to be taken of its content. On the other hand it might be an *advance label* (Tadros 1985: 22–8), indicating that what follows is intended as an odd or amusing anecdote; this would attract the classification M.

The advance label is in a different relationship with its fulfilment than any of the other Ms, or indeed the Os. Whereas an OT is essentially a linking unit, which expresses a relationship between two Ms, one on either side of it, an advance label expresses a relationship between itself and a following M. There is only one instance of an advance label in our material, not enough to require a separate categorisation, but in some discourse varieties these are common, and may provide for a further category of M.

After a lot of discussion we have settled for M. There is some support for this view in the laughter that occurs at the outset of the passage (we removed laughter signs from the transcripts, as explained in Chapter 3). We acknowledge that there are places like this in impromptu text where the classification is not clear-cut, and some trace of the other possibilities may remain within the range of individual interpretation. An element of place-holding is probably part of the reason for the deployment of this phrase, but that could be said of almost any phrase at all, and for us a place-holder is a chunk which does not appear to have any other function apart from maintaining the speaking role for the current speaker. This is all part of the inherent fuzziness of natural language, with its accompanying bumps in output, including blends and contaminations. It is said, of an English civil servant asked to assess the likelihood of an event, that he answered "Prossibly"; we are never in total control.

Lines 11 and 13 are of interactive relevance only: the speaker shows some indecision concerning the way of describing someone, opting for *reporter* in line 12, but surrounding the choice with uncertainty markers. *Some kind of* in line 21 also expresses indetermination, but it also plays a grammatical role, similar to that of the indefinite article, and so in removing it we note this function for possible later use.

The second operation is to remove the MF elements, that is, lines 5, 6, 18 and 30. Lines 5 and 6 are superseded by line 7 which is a new start, and they have no effect on the subsequent discourse; lines 18 and 30 are single words repeated immediately. In neither case do the deletions need to be noted.

Line 9 takes us to the third operation, because it is an MA and only the last half-word needs to be removed. Line 9 is shortly followed by +M (line 10). The two lines are merged by omitting the repeated element.

The third operation is to reconcile M– and following M+ segments. These are first found in lines 10 and 12, which come together when line 11 is removed. Then lines 20–3 give a slightly more complex picture; 21 is removed, and 22 is marked with the double symbol +M–, which indicates that it should be concatenated with

20 and 23 into a single segment. This is an interim position — the resulting string is incoherent — so we must return to the sequence later.

Next we turn to MS, of which there are two instances, at lines 8 and 24. In both cases they provide supplementary information to the immediately preceding element; there is no need for further adjustments to the form before adding them on to the previous line, so line 8 is simply added on to line 7 and line 24 to line 23.

Finally the single MR element at line 15 is merged with the preceding M. The MR element adds *the hunger* to the previous line *he went on strike*. The most natural interpretation of line 15 is simply as a clarifying element. The definite article is not appropriate here, and the two lines can be merged as *he went on hunger strike*.

The revised version contains half the number of lines, which are now recognisable units contributing to the incrementation of shared experience.

(7) b.
1. and — OT
2. it's funny thing — M
3. because — OT
4. it was an article i read — M
5. it was a famous Estonian television reporter — M
6. he went on hunger strike — M
7. because — OT
8. the Estonian government — M
9. they made simplifying towards the citizenship law for the Russians — M
10. so — OT
11. he went to the hunger strike — M
12. because of — OT
13. the(ir) thinking — M
14. that — OT
15. it's unfair — M

This revised version is quite close to the norms of coherent written prose. We can now consider any further adjustments that arise from the analytical process, and offer low level rephrasings where the elements do not fit together harmoniously. The advance label in line 2 is more natural with an indefinite article added, and the second *it was*, in line 5, is a kind of conversational pattern that would appear in written text as *about*; the *he* that begins line 5 is better in written form as *who*; lines 4–6 makes up a unit which now reads:

> *It was an article I read about a famous Estonian television reporter who went on hunger strike.*

The next unit comprises lines 7–9, and *they* at the beginning of line 9 can be omitted;

like line 5, this is a common conversational pattern, whereas in writing it is not normal to follow the subject phrase with a pronoun. Line 11 is almost the same as line 6, but these two lines are too far from each other to constitute a case of MR; in lines 12 to 15 the speaker is providing a further clarification to her explanation of the television reporter's hunger strike — in this sense the element is a return to a previous topic.

The second revision leaves the passage in this form:

(7) c. And it's a funny thing <u>because</u> it was an article | I read | about a famous Estonian television reporter | who went on hunger strike <u>because</u> the Estonian government | made simplifying towards the citizenship law | for the Russians — <u>so</u> he went on hunger strike <u>because of</u> the(ir) thinking <u>that</u> it's unfair.

This is fairly easy to understand, but we can introduce a few improvements on an ad hoc basis to improve the coherence. Line 3, *because*, is characteristic of spoken language — there is no need for a cause/effect relationship to be explicit here, and we interpret the "funniness" of the anecdote that follows to be a personal judgement of the speaker. The M unit, *It was an article I read* is a transformation of *I read an article*, with a particular focus on *article*. A topic introducing focus of this kind is characteristic of informal conversation, but not necessary here, so we can express this phrase in the unmarked form. The phrase *made simplifying towards* is poor in terms of Standard English, partly because of the speaker's command of the language and partly because of changes that have been made around it; a better expression would be *made a simplification of*. The pronouns and verb tenses now get a little mixed, and it is helpful to replace *it's* by *the law was*.

We return to the problematic *the(ir)*. To interpret it as *their* seems strange because it is the reporter who thinks the situation unfair; however, the preceding discussion has dealt with Estonians' attitudes to Russians, and the indistinctly articulated *the(ir)* could either be the definite article indicating 'the (way of) thinking', or could even be interpreted as 'their' as a group term referring to Estonians more generally. However, the latter is less plausible, which leaves us two possibilities: to maintain it despite its deviation from Standard English, or omit it in the interest of normalisation. Since we have been following the practice of deviating as little as possible from the original text, we decided to keep it as *the*.

With all these revisions incorporated, the passage now reads:

(7) d. *And it's a funny thing because I read an article about a famous Estonian television reporter who went on hunger strike because the Estonian government made a simplification of the citizenship law for the Russians — so he went on hunger strike because of the thinking the law was unfair.*

This long sentence is now a starter for a conventional grammar. It still has something of the informal spoken idiom at the beginning, but it should be able to be handled in a normal grammar. It has come a long way from the original transcription, but the gains and losses have been carefully assessed along the way, and distortion has been kept to a minimum.

In the process of this final synthesis, the interactive elements, the OI, have largely been relegated to notes. Much of the import of those notes remains without further development, even though we have pointed out that the functional demarcation roles are not absolute, and the OI elements can have relevance to the emerging shared knowledge.

We do not think that interactive elements are unimportant, quite the contrary. The OI play an important conversational role in building up shared understanding between participants. This understanding has a wider sense than the actual knowledge incrementation, which is covered by the elements we call M and which we have described as incrementing shared experience: throughout any conversation, interactants are constructing mutual relations, negotiating positions, and relating to or distancing themselves from the topics or each other. Such elements are part of the shared experience, even though their structural relevance is immediately lost. This is a substantial area of language study which is not our first priority in this book, and we concede that further work is necessary to tie up the loose ends.

The main focus of our present work is to bridge the gap between text and grammar by introducing a new point of departure for grammatical analysis. We believe that this is an angle which is equally fruitful for delving deeper into interaction, and that by making this our starting point we can maintain a holistic view of language which integrates its diverse resources of expression. The interactive side of spoken discourse has been very thoroughly explored in the last thirty years, and a different perspective is now worth considering.

Section C

Theory and follow-up

CHAPTER 10

The example texts analysed

Throughout the book and especially when presenting the steps in our analytical approach we have been illustrating our points with the help of six text extracts whose selection and characteristics were described in Chapter 3. We felt that it was necessary to gather the extracts in one place and set out the analysis that we have assigned to them, since not every line is discussed in the individual methodological descriptions. It is also perhaps more illuminating to see longer continuous stretches of text analysed with the same apparatus.

In the development of the descriptive system we studied and categorised much longer stretches of text than those chosen to illustrate the system; but for the workshops and now for publication we chose shorter extracts for most careful attention so that the various analytic decisions could be presented clearly but without too much detail.

We also wanted to comment on the texts, because we realised during our analysis and especially in the process of writing this up that the analyses showed interesting differences between the texts. The analysis had thrown some well-known features of some texts into relief — such as the presence of fragments in speech, but also some that were less obvious, like the variation of chunk size between texts. It is an interesting and very likely a useful feature of the present system that it can differentiate between types of text. Many other models do this, of course, but since detecting text typological differences was not among our objectives in initiating this project, this was a pleasant surprise.

So in this chapter we go through each of the texts in approximately the order in which we carried out the analyses, though the *Gazetteer* text, which we place last both here and in Chapter 3, became part of the project at an earlier stage.

Lexis

This is the first text sample that was analysed, and one of the first texts to be recorded and transcribed as part of an electronic corpus. The text, as archived, is a stream of alphabetic characters and spaces, without punctuation and all in upper case. There is no indication of change of speaker, nor of how many speakers there are. It was interesting to us because it is about as minimal a text as one can imagine. For the sake of the comments below, we have added possible speaker assignments on the basis of two speakers, but we have no evidence for this other than the text itself. A reader who disagrees with our assignments will also interpret the sequence of events somewhat differently; while diverse opinions will affect the perception of the discourse structure, it is remarkable how little they affect the final LUMs.

1.	A	IT	MF
2.		WE	MF
3.		WE CROSSED TO DENMARK	M
4.		IN THE MORNING	MS
5.		I REMEMBER	OI
6.		FROM HAMBURG TO GEDSER	MS
7.		I THINK	OI
8.		A PLACE CALLED GEDSER	MR
9.	B	OH YES	OI
10.	A	IN DENMARK	M
11.		WE CROSSED IN THE MORNING	M
12.	B	THE FRONTIER	M
13.		YOU MEAN	OI
14.	A	YES YES	OI
15.		AND THEN	OT
16.		IT WASNT VERY INTERESTING IN DENMARK	M
17.		BECAUSE	OT
18.		FIRST OF ALL	OT
19.		IT WAS POURING WITH RAIN	M
20.	B	OH DEAR	OI
21.	A	ABSOLUTELY POURING WITH RAIN	MR
22.	B	HA	OI
23.	A	YES	OI
24.		SO	OT
25.		I DIDNT REALLY ENJOY BEING ON THE BOAT	M
26.		BUT	OT
27.		THE SCENERYS VERY FLAT	M
28.		I SUPPOSE	OI
29.	B	IS IT	OI

This passage is one of impromptu conversation, and so we can be fairly sure that OI elements will figure prominently. We do not expect the same density of them in carefully considered written prose; when they occur there they are likely to be representations of speech, such as dialogue in novels and stories, more indications of informality than any kind of interactional control. See below for an example of literary use of OI elements. If they are prominent in ordinary written prose then their superfluousness becomes obvious — some writing intended for children is of this nature, and it is sometimes found in attempts by bureaucracies to make their procedures understandable.

In this extract the speakers combine to make a narrative, with one telling the story and the other supporting and encouraging. There are thus quite a few OI elements because the interaction needs to be managed; some from the narrator in order to keep the floor, and some from the supporter to indicate a lively interest in the story. The lead speaker dominates the talk, if the speaker changes have been correctly interpreted, and the longest contribution from the supporter is of four words, early in the extract, suggesting that the supporter gives up any attempt at a constructive role.

There is little indication that the supporter would prefer a more balanced turn-taking, and at one point the narrator makes it pretty clear that the floor is not for yielding. At line 12 the supporter says *the frontier, you mean*, the only supporting utterance with any lexical content, in the word *frontier*. The narrator immediately counters with *yes yes*, which could be anything from dismissive to impatient, but certainly retrieves the conversational initiative promptly on the only occasion that a challenge might have been mounted.

This exchange is also interesting because we interpret line 12 as a continuation of the narrator's utterance. Without the intonation for guidance we cannot be sure if it is a full yes/no question or rather, as we see it, a clarification with which the narrator is expected to concur. None of the other contributions from the supporter challenge the narrator even as far as asking for information; they are all pure supports — line 9, *Oh yes* is simple concurrence, line 20 is emotional concurrence, and the last line, which could also be a yes/no question, is interpreted as a sympathetic supportive tag, and not a question at all. So the supporter is really devoted to supporting, and adding little or nothing to the shared experience of the speakers. All that comes from the narrator.

This is a characteristic passage of informal story-telling. The selected, possibly self-selected storyteller holds forth, and the other participants confine themselves mainly to audience reaction that brings out aspects of the story, and never challenges it for attention. The narrator, though dominant, is not bullying, and it is clear that on several occasions the supporter declines the option of taking a full turn, and thus diverting the story.

The informality is shown for example in the two MR units, where a perfectly clear statement is rephrased for effect. The poise of the narrator and the restraint of the supporter are shown in the lack of M– units or MF after the very first two lines. Once launched, this is a fluent narrator. The rather few OT units also suggests fluency; narration is a simple task and — as we see in children — the OTs can tend to become a monotonous succession of "and then"s, of which there is only one in this passage. This suggests that the narrator has at least an outline plan in mind for the story, and little need of actual constructive help from the supporter. However, when both participants seem to lose interest in the story, as in the last few lines of this passage, it is the supporter who, in the utterance that immediately follows line 29, rekindles the story with a strong elicitation: *Yes tell me what happens when….*

This is, on the whole, a neat conversation, quite well structured and performed competently by the participants. It did not warn us of the less orderly events that we would turn to in our later samples.

The neatness comes out in several ways that have not been mentioned as yet. One is that there is no recorded overlapping; another is that whatever the distribution of turns among speakers this is less important than the co-operative construction of shared experience, and the co-operation is very clear here. Thirdly, the passage is very easily handled in Step Five, and falls neatly into coherent consecutive units. Lines 1–8 are merged as one of the examples in Step Five (Chapter 9), and the remainder is just as easy:

> . . . *a place called Gedser in Denmark. We crossed the frontier in the morning* <u>but</u> *it wasn't very interesting in Denmark because first of all it was absolutely pouring with rain,* <u>and</u> *so I really didn't enjoy being on the boat;* <u>also</u> *the scenery's very flat.*

There are three OT items added (underlined above) to enable the written form to flow; they are substituted for *and then, ha yes,* and *but* respectively. The weak *and then* is replaced by *but* because there is an expectation of interest in each stage of a narrative about a journey; *ha* and *yes* are two OI units which make an interactive pair, and the *so* that follows is another example of the narrator making sure of the floor; these interactive sequences have to be smoothed out in the final version. The *but* seems odd unless very flat scenery is to one's liking; *because* might be more to the point but that would be an unjustified addition to the meaning; the neutral *also* keeps up the flow, adding very little.

ELFA

This extract comes from a conversation with altogether seven participants who use English as a lingua franca in a university seminar session. The sample is from a discussion following a presentation, and the main speakers here are native speakers of Dutch and Lithuanian, with one backchannelling remark from a Finnish speaker.

This is the whole extract with its analysis.

1.	A:	yeah	OI
2.		but	OT
3.		ca-	MF
4.		can i legally	M–
5.		if i'm a Russian	+M–
6.		living in Estonia	MS
7.		like	OI
8.		(if) i don't speak Estonian	M–
9.		can i legally open a shop	+M
10.		or	OT
11.		er	OI
12.		work at this shop	+M
13.	B:	you have to use their	MF
14.		you have to use their language	M
15.		even in business	MS
16.		it's	MF
17.		it's law now	M
18.	C:	yeah	OI
19.	B:	you have to use it	M
20.		if you can't	MF
21.		if you can't prove	M–
22.		that	OT
23.		you have the sufficient	+MF
24.		well	OI
25.		that's what i believe	OI
26.		if you don't have	MF
27.		that	OT
28.		you have a sufficient	M–
29.		er	OI
30.		knowledge	+M–
31.	A:	yeah	OI
32.	B:	of Estonian	MS
33.		then	OT
34.		you can't do	MF
35.	A:	then	OT
36.		you can't even get a job	M
37.		officially	MS
38.	B:	well	OI

39.		i think	OI
40.		in certain areas	M–
41.		you can	+M
42.		but	OT
43.		for example	OT
44.		in service	M–
45.		you can't	+M
46.		if you have to	MF
47.	A:	mhm	OI
48.	B:	erm	OI
49.		if you have a direct contact	M–
50.		with the people	+M
51.		and	OT
52.		you don't have	M–
53.		s–	MF
54.		efficient Estonian	+M
55.		then	OT
56.		you can't get it	M
57.	A:	yeah yeah	OI
58.		okay	OI
59.	B:	and	OT
60.		i mean	OI
61.		it's funny thing	M
62.		because	OT
63.		the	MF
64.		the Estonian	MF
65.		it was an article	M
66.		i read	MS
67.		it was a famous Estonian tele-	MA
68.		television	+M–
69.		i don't know	OI
70.		reporter	+M
71.		or something	OI
72.		he went on strike	M
73.		on the hunger strike	MR
74.		because	OT
75.		er	OI
76.		the	MF
77.		the Estonian government	M
78.		they made	M–

79.	some kind of	OI
80.	simplifying	+M−
81.	towards the citizenship law	+M
82.	for the Russians	MS
83.	so	OT
84.	he went to the hunger strike	M
85.	because of	OT
86.	the(ir) thinking	M
87.	that	OT
88.	it's	MF
89.	it's unfair	M

Although this is spontaneous speaking, the individual units are relatively long, their average length being among the longest in our sample. One might expect academic talk to feature longish phrases on account of referential complexity alone (*the citizenship law*), but other things also contribute to the impression of length and complexity in this text. There are quite a few MS units (message supplements), which provide specifications or expansions to the preceding M unit, and have the effect of chaining increments into larger wholes.

B, who does most of the talking, uses long turns. The longest comprises all of thirty segments, spanning lines 59 to 89, where the turn and the extract end. The long turns also enhance the feeling of complexity, since they are made up of different kinds of elements. Coherence in long and complex turns can be managed with the help of text-oriented organising elements (OT), and in contrast to the other spoken extracts, this text has a high number of OT units.

However, even though both length and complexity are apparent in the extract, it is at the same time also fragmentary, with several MF units. Clearly, speaking a foreign language is taxing on processing capacity, and a certain degree of fragmentariness is only to be expected. It is equally clear though, that the speakers here are strongly oriented to the content — in the broadest sense, that is, to making points and making sense of each other's contributions. Most of the fragments are followed by the speakers' immediate self-rephrasing, which together with the long turns gives the speech a feel of determination and goal-orientedness despite some processing difficulty.

Even though most message fragments are rephrased by the speaker, there is one place (lines 35–7) where A completes B's fragment. It was A's question which elicited the response from B in the first place, and at the point where A performs the completion the answer seems by and large to have taken shape. Yet after the collaborative completion, B continues on a slightly different tack, as if to correct A's completion where it had gone a little far: A interprets B's response to mean that it is not possible to get a job in Estonia without proof that you speak Estonian well enough, but B begins to qualify that interpretation. She goes on to elaborate on the matter until line 56, and ends with a generalisation in lines 49–56. Again the exchange gives the impression of a strong orientation towards content and purpose by both parties.

The speakers give each other feedback and use a fair amount of backchannelling, as speakers normally do. It has been noted, however, that L2 conversations have a particularly high incidence of comprehension signalling such as backchannelling (Kurhila 2003; Mauranen 2006). This is also one of the interactive features which clearly marks this extract as spoken interaction, despite the evident content orientation. A notable proportion of the units are interactive, and although some are filled pauses serving to keep the floor (*er, erm*), many convey attitudinal stances (*well, I think, I don't know, it's funny thing*).

In this extract, we can also see the brief lifespan of a topic increment, observed in Chapter 8. In line 46, B starts an if-clause increment, which she interrupts despite A's encouragement (*mmm*, line 47), hesitates, and starts again with an *if*-clause in line 49. The latter *if*-clause increment is continued by the next unit (+M, line 50), but although its logical conclusion *then* (54) and *you can't get it* (56) follow in the same turn, line 56 is too far from the *if* increment to be taken as a continuation of this unit. It is a new increment, even though it very clearly continues topics already taken up earlier in the discourse; *get it* for example resumes the earlier topic of getting a job.

We had access to the soundtrack of this extract, which enabled us to check the accuracy of the transcription, but the only place where the soundtrack resolved a potential ambiguity of interpretation was *that* in line 27: if it had been stressed, we would have been likely to place it at the end of line 26, as part of that unit, but since it was unstressed, we analysed it as a separate unit, as an OT. In fact *have* in the previous line looks very much like a somewhat unhappy lexical choice; the unit echoes the earlier unit in line 21 (*if you can't prove*), which begins the speaker's first attempt at formulating the answer to A's question. But shortly after this B interrupts herself by two OI units modifying the certainty of her assertion (*well, that's what I believe*), and then resumes the discourse, but falters a little in the second round of making her point, which A reformulates for her (lines 35–7).

On the whole, this extract reflects its academic origin in manifesting both length and complexity compared to the other spoken texts, while it is also distinct from the written texts in having a good proportion of interactive elements. It also shows traces of being a foreign language text with its high number of message fragments. The situational context of a seminar discussion seems to give the text a strong orientation towards content, together with a drive towards finishing points; this is not a chatty piece, even if it is interactive.

HKCSE

The extract is from the Hong Kong Corpus of Spoken English, part of an informal conversation in a restaurant between two women, one of whom is a native speaker of English and the other a Hong Kong Chinese speaker of English as a second language.

1.	A:	yea	OI
2.	B:	deep-fried pork chop	M
3.	A:	yea	OI
4.	B:	and then	OT
5.		with the oil	M–
6.		butter	MR
7.		um	OI
8.		the	MF
9.		I	MF
10.		I'm not sure	OI
11.		it must be	M–
12.	A:	kind of mushroom	+M
13.	B:	it's a kind of mushroom	MR
14.	A:	the Japanese mushroom	MR
15.		okay okay	OI
16.		I know	OI
17.		I know	OI
18.		the	MF
19.		the long thin white one	M
20.		right	OI
21.	B:	yes	OI
22.		the long thin white one	MR
23.	A:	uhuh	OI
24.	B:	yea	OI
25.		and then	OT
26.		the other one is	MA
27.		um er	OI
28.		is the rice	+M
29.		um	OI
30.		like	OI
31.		the	MF
32.		I think	OI
33.		it's the	MA

34.	sort of	OI
35.	the roast beefs	+M

This is a brief extract where the length of the units varies a good deal. What particularly characterises this dialogue is the dominance of interactive units: nearly half of all the units are OI, and in fact if we had opted for narrower chunking this would have produced a couple more. In all, we can say that half of this extract is interactive speech, and in this respect it stands out among the texts. The interactive units mostly constitute brief exchanges between the speakers (as in lines 20–1, or 23–4 for instance), while some serve to maintain the floor (*um, er, like*) and others to express stance (*I'm not sure, I know, I think*). The strong feeling of interactiveness is further enhanced by the MR (message replacement) units, which are done collaboratively, all but one (line 6, where the speaker replaces her own M– unit); in line 11 B *says it must be*, which is an incomplete message unit (M–), collaboratively completed by A, who offers *a kind of mushroom*. Then B accepts it by expanding this a little (line 13), and finally A specifies the mushroom once more (line 14). A similar exchange takes place in lines 19 to 22, beginning with A's *the long thin white one*, followed by an exchange of OI units and B's verbatim reproduction of *the long thin white one* — and once again, an exchange of OI units follows. The interactive behaviour of these two speakers seems to highlight cooperativeness quite conspicuously.

The number of message fragments (MF) is also relatively high in this extract, which one would expect in spoken text, and perhaps also in a dialogue where one of the participants is a non-native speaker. It must be noted, though, that the fragments do not only appear in the non-native speech, nor are fragments by any means absent from the native speaker dialogue (*Lexis*) that is also in our sample. It is clear from previous research that fragments characterise speaking in contrast to written text (e.g. Levelt 1989; Biber et al. 1999), and are very similar in native and non-native speakers (Mauranen forthcoming a).

One message type that makes no appearance in this text is the MS, message supplement, which elaborates a previous M unit. The absence of MS units to contributes to a sense that this text is not very complex. Clearly, message-supplementing increments elaborate the message they follow and thereby make the evolving meaning complex. Without a single such increment, the discourse appears fairly simple and not particularly content-oriented, despite the units being relatively long. Turns are short, and thus both speakers get a good chance of speaking, even though altogether B speaks about twice as much as A.

The speakers make use of deictic reference several times (*the oil, the other one, the rice, the roast beefs*). They proceed sequentially (*and then* organising the activity in lines 4 and 25), as if working out a solution to a task. There thus seems to be a shared tactical goal, in the pursuit of which speaking plays a role, and which guides the conversation. In contrast, in the ELFA text the entire situation consists in speaking, and spoken exchanges carry the whole burden of success.

One interesting thing about this extract is that the scholars who supplied us with the sample, Professors Warren and Cheng, compared our chunks with their own analysis into tone units, and found that they were closely aligned. The close correspondence supports the perceptions of various scholars who have used phonological units as "chunks" (see Chapter 2), but it also supports our reliance on the intuitive perceptions of ourselves and others. Warren and Cheng (pers. comm.) also reported support for the basic distinction between O and M units, finding that backchannel moves did not occur immediately following O units and tended to occur at the end of completed M units.

In all, the extract gives the impression of being a relaxed and fairly simple exchange between very cooperative interlocutors. The interaction comes across as more central than the precise content of the exchange. In contrast to the academic ELFA with its long turns and elaborate messages, this text is not so argumentative nor so strictly shaped around a pre-determined goal, although the participants appear to be engaged in cooperative activity which the speech accompanies.

The Independent

This text was chosen for analysis to represent a text which would be as 'normal' as possible: expository written prose from a conventionally respectable source. We felt that a broadsheet newspaper editorial is an ordinary, normal text. The particular extract was selected simply to correspond to our notion of a prototypical editorial: a comment on domestic politics.

This is the extract in its analysed form:

1. Mr Kennedy   M—
2. now   OT
3. declares   +M—
4. that   OT
5. it must be   M–
6. bold   +M
7. in its thinking   MS
8. and   OT
9. ready to plan   MS
10. long-term.   MS
11. Sounding nice   M–

12.	is no longer enough,	+M
13.	he argued.	M
14.	From now on,	M–
15.	the Liberal Democrats	+M–
16.	have to present themselves	+M
17.	as a party	+M
18.	that wants power	MS
19.	and	OT
20.	knows	MS–
21.	what it wants to do	+M
22.	if it gets it.	MS
23.	With that in mind,	OT
24.	he announced	M–
25.	two reviews,	+M
26.	one	OT
27.	to take a broad look	M–
28.	at policy,	+M
29.	the other	OT
30.	to look at	M–
31.	tax policy,	+M
32.	as well as	OT
33.	a number of	M–
34.	internal reviews	+M
35.	into the party's structure	MS
36.	and	OT
37.	communications.	MS

Because this text is an editorial which comments on another text, a speech given by Charles Kennedy, it works at two levels simultaneously, incorporating two speaker voices. The first level is the basic writer-reader relationship, where the writer addresses the reader and essentially assumes normal responsibility for his or her own words. The other level consists of the editor representing Kennedy, that is paraphrasing Kennedy and writing on his behalf.

We as readers have no way of knowing what Kennedy might have said originally, we only have access to it via the text that the editor has written. What Kennedy really said is of course not the point of the text and is not immediately in our interests to discover: the editorial genre presents the editor's interpretation of an event or previous discourse, it is free to represent them from the editor's point of view and we as readers are expected to read it as such.

What we have in this text is thus two intertwining voices, one which is the direct address acting as a kind of outer shell of the text, and the indirect address where the editor is paraphrasing Kennedy, or assuming Kennedy's perspective.

The O and M elements are for the most part ambiguous in terms of the two writer roles the editor assumes: as editor and as Kennedy. For example in line 13 the editor makes a separation between himself (or herself) and Kennedy (*he argued*), but to what extent the summary of what Kennedy argued corresponds to his original wording is not known. More intriguingly, the editor assumes an omniscient role in reporting what Kennedy's intentions were (*with that in mind*, line 23), and we are at a complete loss to infer what the status of the reported intention is — is this reporting what Kennedy said his intention had been, or is it the editor's conjecture?

As written text, the extract stands on its own, with no need to consult a soundtrack or a video of the writer working away at a computer; it is at home in the mode it is expressed in, and needs little help from either layout or typography. As written text, it has no MF elements, which gives the impression that it is not fragmentary but constitutes a lucid whole.

What characterises this text is the overwhelming dominance of M elements of different kinds: there is in fact only one plain M, all the others anticipate a continuance (M–), fulfil anticipation (M+) or add to a preceding element (MS). The extract is thus heavily message-oriented, as we might expect from an editorial, and also complex, weaving an intricate network of interrelated message elements. This feel of complexity is also supported by the shortness of the segments; what we have here are short but interrelated M increments. Although the length of segments might be expected to typify serious written prose, in this case length does not a feature of the increments but at a higher level, where the writer divides up his or her own text in sentences. The whole extract of 89 words is made up of only four sentences, one rather short, and it is the three longer ones that give the impression of length.

Another distinctive feature of this text is an abundant use of OTs, of which it has more than any other text in the sample. The presence of many textual organisers enhances the impression of complexity, since these assume the task of navigating the reader through the many brief increments and the different stages of the argument.

This text is not overtly interactive: there are no OI elements at all. This fact is likely to contribute to the common understanding of serious non-literary written prose as being self-contained and objective. Even though there is a strong sense of intertextuality, as the constant presence of two voices discussed above indicates, and even though the text takes a clear stance, it also maintains a sense of detachment, which manifests itself in the absence of overt contact with or mention of the reader.

In all, this text consists of brief, interrelated increments, which are organised by a number of text-organising devices. Although its self-chosen units, i.e. sentences, are long, this is not the case with its message increments. As a text which has been written with the purpose of being read from a newspaper, it also fits its context and mode snugly, and gives the appearance of being very 'normal' and appropriate. It also conveys a sense of being autonomous in having no overt markers of interaction.

Joyce

In the second half of our research, when we felt that the evolving system of analysis was coping well with a range of informal spoken transcripts, we decided to widen the range of texts, and to include a literary one. We were interested in the "stream of consciousness" kind of writing, which to some extent seems to model itself on informal spoken styles, and we thought that it might be interesting to compare authentic speech with the fabricated variety.

In James Joyce's novel *Ulysses*, at the beginning of her famous "monologue", the author creates the semblance of Molly Bloom making a character assassination of another character, Mrs. Riordan.

1.	I hope	M–
2.	I'll never be	+M–
3.	like her	+M
4.	a wonder	M–
5.	she didn't want us	+M–
6.	to cover	+M–
7.	our faces	+M
8.	but	OI
9.	she was	M–
10.	a welleducated woman	+M
11.	certainly	OI
12.	and	OI
13.	her gabby talk	M
14.	about Mr Riordan here	MS
15.	and	OT
16.	Mr Riordan there	MS
17.	I suppose	M–
18.	he was glad	+M–
19.	to get shut of her	+M
20.	and	OT
21.	her dog	M

22.	smelling my fur	MS
23.	and	OT
24.	always	M–
25.	edging to get up	+M
26.	under my petticoats	+M
27.	especially then	OI
28.	still	OI
29.	I like that in him	M
30.	polite to old women	MS
31.	like that	MS
32.	and	OT
33.	waiters	MS
34.	and	OT
35.	beggars	MS
36.	too	OT

Just a list of how many of each type of chunk occur in this passage is revealing:

OT	6
OI	5
M	3
MF	0
M–	5
+M	6
+M–	4
MS	7
MR	0
MA	0

The total number of O elements, at 11 in 36, is quite a high density even for spoken text, and of course we would not expect any OI in written material. But on the other hand, the complete absence of MF, MA and MR indicate carefully planned rather than impromptu language; no change of phrasing, no hesitations. Informal speech is unlikely to keep going for very long without one or other of these coming in.

There are only three simple Ms, so the greater majority of the M elements are either incomplete (9 instances) or they complete or extend the LUM (17 instances). In particular the large number of MS elements may be intended to give the impression of afterthoughts rather than planned speech. The last seven segments, for example, are just tacked onto each other without prospection, and also 21–6.

Part of the impression created by stream of consciousness writing is that the "speaker" is not in full control of what she or he is saying, and the words tend to pour out; lots of MS elements will help to create this impression. Also an M– is always immediately followed by +M or +M–; Os are not interpolated here, unlike much spontaneous speech. This means that the general flow of the text is of the *release* type (Sinclair 1972b and forthcoming) and is not *arrested*. The absence of punctuation is a simple but effective way of creating the impression of speech tumbling out, because the reader, accustomed to being provided with punctuation, has to work it out, thus engaging with matters of *completeness* (see Chapter 11), which are normally the responsibility of the author.

In considering a simulated speech event in a literary text, we can envisage two different analyses: one analysis accepts the passage "straight" and assumes that it is written by James Joyce for the reader; for most third-person narrative there is no textual indication otherwise, but in this case there are the speech-type indications to be accounted for. The text is known to have no direct basis in the spoken word, and even if Joyce's natural speech patterns were of this kind there is no explanation for why he changes from the normal written style of most novels.

The other interpretation adds the "suspension of disbelief" that literary authors frequently rely on, and analyses the passage as if it were the transcript of a real monologue. The second position, though more complicated, is the only viable one because it is the only one that explains the observed linguistic phenomena. Under the conventions of *free indirect speech*, the author gives indications of the likely "voice" of one of the characters, and then can create speech situations like a puppeteer.

So unlike all the other analyses in this book, this one is influenced by literary conventions. For example line 12, *and* is labelled OI, where the other *and*s are labelled OT. This decision is made because the analyst, imagining how the words might have been uttered, thinks that the word is not a textual co-ordinator, but is a discourse place-holder which served to tag on the next few segments simply as a concatention. With a grammatical *and* one would expect the syntax following the word to mirror the preceding syntax, because like is co-ordinated to like, but there is no equivalent to line 9 *she was* in the following segments.

This judgement can only be made in the world of fiction, because we know that it was created by James Joyce sitting at his desk thinking himself into the kind of situation he was simulating. The analysis is equally imaginative, and so the OI attributed to line 12 is a fictional OI, just as the text is fictional.

Another example could be line 27, *especially then*. Here the impression given is of afterthought — having said lines 24–6 Molly reflects on what she has just said; Lines 28 and 29 continue in the same way, as Molly switches her attention, without warning, from the lady with the dog to — presumably — Mr Riordan. If this was a monologue which was unfolding in real time these lines would be seen as an impromptu reaction of Molly to her own speech, which could not possibly be planned. Within the narrative of *Ulysses*, of course, it is crafted to give that impression.

The general conclusion to commentary on this passage is that it adopts some of the characteristic patterns of speech, but only some of them, so it is quite distinct from actual monologue (see Burton 1980 on the contrast between drama dialogue and real dialogue). It also gives priority to constructions like MS that create the impression of frequent additions to complete constructions, and OI elements that simulate impromptuness in a highly considered piece.

The Gazetteer

The final text is an entry from Pear's Cyclopedia, 1985. It is included to be representative of a highly specialised variety of English, in this case Written English. The experience of reading it and understanding it is rather similar to the interpretation task that was offered in the Preamble to this book — after a few seconds it becomes clear that there are special conventions to this kind of language, and that there are repetitive sequences of statements. There is some guidance on interpretation given at the beginning of the section, on pages K2 and K3, but we make the assumption that most readers do not consult this information, finding that they can make sufficient sense of the text without it.

1. **Malaysia**, M
2. **Federation of**, MS
3. indep. federation M
4. (1963), MS
5. S. E. **Asia**; M
6. member of Brit. Commonwealth; M
7. inc. W. Malaysia M
8. (Malaya) MS
9. and OT
10. E. Malaysia M
11. (Borneo sts. of Sarawak and Sabah); MS
12. cap. Kuala Lumpur; M
13. a. 334,110 km^2; M
14. p. (est.1983) 14,744,000 M

There is just one O element in this passage, and of the range of M elements, only M and MS are used, making it a text of very simple structure and highly distinctive. At this first stage of generalisation, however, the unusual nature of the language of the text is obscured, and its difference from ordinary written prose appears only in a restricted selection of the structural options.

Because there are hardly any O elements, there is hardly any control of the relationship between writer and reader, nor of the relationship between each textual segment and the next. The assumption must be that in each case the relationship is obvious. The obviousness is helped, as in many similar publications, by the existence of a rigorous paragraph structure, so that, for example, lines 12, 13 and 14 always come in that sequence. Also they, and most of the others, simply accumulate information. The only difference is that some of them, those marked MS, tack extra information onto a previously complete segment.

Let us examine the postulate that the paragraph structure is predetermined and rigid. The entry after this one deals with West Malaysia, one of the constituent territories of the Federation of Malaysia; there is no equivalent to line 12 in this entry, and the line preceding 13 is *35 percent of p. Chinese*. This is followed by the equivalent of lines 13 and 14, concerning the area and population of the country respectively.

35 per cent of p. Chinese; a. 131,588 km^2; p. (1968) 8,899,000.

The sequence would be most unusual in an ordinary paragraph in English. It would be natural for the total population figure to be given before the more specific point about the number of Chinese in the population — since it is a percentage it is dependent on the total figure for full interpretation. The statement about the area would surely not be interposed between these two statements about population.

It thus seems likely that there are many hidden rules of sequencing in the underlying paragraph structure, and they are followed regardless of what might be a more natural information flow. In a normal prose paragraph the above example would be taken as a lack of coherence, but in the Gazetteer the two items concerning population have different status; the first is a statement in the political section, which is an optional section not found in most entries, while the total population estimate is a required element in all similar entries, and it has a fixed position.

If the LUMS in the Gazetteer as a whole are either M or MS, as it seems to be from cursory inspection, then the reader never prospects ahead on the basis of what is inside the LUMs. That is to say, the text makes no use of one of the most powerful structural properties available to it, and the main relation of statements to each other is via the paragraph structure, where the fixed sequence of events leads to some possible prospection.

The PUBs fall into place, following those punctuation marks which are not indications of abbreviation, and before some, but not all, opening brackets. One bracketed element, in the last line, remains within the segment because it is a fixed part of the structure of all such lines; the structure is:

p. (est. [date]) [number])

There are thus two uses of round brackets in the text, at different places in structure. At the level of LUMs, a bracketed segment denotes a separate LUM, while within the structure of an M which begins with *p.*, the bracketed segment is integral to that structure. In the real world, population figures are always estimates, and without the date of the estimate the figure is almost meaningless.

Internally, the Ms have one, two or three elements of quasi-clause structure; in the case of one-element lines, (1 — 6 and 8, 10, 11) each is dependent on a convention that governs the interpretation of such texts — each piece of information is interpreted as adding to the features and qualities of the headword and what is to be expected in the way of information from this kind of text, and what is the anticipated sequence of presentation, as evidenced by all the other entries. See Chapter 12 for an explanation of units with a single element.

So line 1 states the "headword" or topic of the entry, in bold face; an accepted convention of dictionaries and other reference works. Line 2 is also in bold, signifying that it is an extension of the headword; the unusual syntax, ending in *of*, is part of the distinctive style of this variety and some others, like formal catalogues and inventories. Line 3 gives the status of Malaysia and line 4 gives the year in which it acquired that status. Line 5 indicates its geographical location; the word *Asia* is in bold print, to indicate the larger region, in this case a continent, in which Malaysia lies. This is consistent with other entries — a town, for instance, will be followed by the name of its country in bold face. Then follows its political affiliation in line 6, and the component territories of the Federation (lines 7–11).

In each case from line 3 onwards we interpret the single M as adding more information about Malaysia, directly in the case of lines 3, 6 and 10, and via a previous M in the cases of lines 4, 8 and 11. The MS assignment for these last three lines indicates that the route for interpretation is indirect. The sequence of information, headword, expansion of headword, political status, date of acquiring political status, geographical location, political affiliation, constituency — this follows a regular pattern in all similar entries.

The Ms which are made up of two elements of structure are lines 7, 12 and 13. In each case the first unit is chosen from the special vocabulary of the Gazetteer, and the second supplies relevant information about it; it is essentially an "attribute-value" structure, and the attributes, such as *cap. a.* and *p.* here, are explained in a list of abbreviations on page K3 of the Cyclopedia. The attribute *inc.* in line 7 has a list as its value, here lines 8 — 11. The value is thus related to the headword via the attribute.

The single instance of a line with three elements of structure is the last line, which is an "attribute-value" line with an added bracketed element, already explained.

As pointed out above, there is a sole instance of *and* as an OT in the passage; a marginal case, given the lack of explicit structural guidance, but one that shows an uncommon feature of "Gazetteer language". In Gazetteer language each piece of information has one of the three types of structure just illustrated; so everything after *inc.* in line 8 up to the end of line 10 is just one informational element. However, *inc.* is one of the rather rare instances of prospection in this variety, because *inc.* has a tendency to propect more than one item of information, and so additionally prospects *and*.

Later in this book (Chapter 12) there is a discussion of the difficulties experienced by traditional methods of language description when faced with passages of this kind. LUMs would first be paraphrased into clauses which had finite verbs and added articles and determiners, everything needed to improve the explicitness of the structures. The resultant paraphrase would then assigned a structure, one which had in fact been added in the act of paraphrasing; the aberrant phrase was thus assimilated into the regular grammar of the language. However, this process obscured the fact that a competent user of the language is able to interpret the passage with little effort, and probably without recourse to the list of abbreviations. That is, the text itself, unaltered, creates the necessary meaning. Further, it would not be possible for an accurate paraphrase to be made unless the original text had been clearly understood.

The ability of LUG to assign relationships by examining the boundaries rather than the internal relationships, and the strategies for deriving meaning from single-unit LUMs are advantages not open to conventional grammars. Further analysis such as that suggested in Chapter 12 will further explain the way in which this divergent variety makes its meaning.

In the light of this argument it is not very helpful to put the *Gazetteer* through Step Five. The reason is that it is such a specialised variety, of the kind called a *sublanguage* many years ago; as such it recognises and makes use of two types of pattern that are not found in the general language:

1. There are lexical items and syntactic structures that are not found in the general language, like *p.* and *Federation of*; also typographical conventions like bold face that have special meanings like "continent" in the case of **Asia** in our sample text.
2. There are patterns of organisation at the paragraph level that are unique to the structure of an entry, and guide the interpretation.

To replace these with appropriate expressions in ordinary English would run the risk of giving approval to the paraphrasing that has been criticised as hiding the failure of conventional grammars to tackle the specific ways in which this kind of text makes its meaning. The paraphrasing is trivially easy, and there are endless possible ways of representing this meaning in ordinary English.

It would be vastly preferable to automate this step, in order to show that the meaning is already interpreted before the text is paraphrased. The automation, though simple, is beyond the scope of this book, but characteristic of the kind of small local grammars that are multiplying in the field of text mining.

CHAPTER 11

Theoretical synopsis

In this chapter we present a summary of the essential theoretical arguments we have been developing in this book, pointing out connections to influential developments in linguistic thinking. We also outline here the import of this new position to further perspectives on language theory.

When the study of spoken discourse began, analysts concentrated quite naturally on its greatest novelty as compared with written language, which had been the bedrock of structural studies for centuries. The way in which two or more participants could create a coherent and meaningful experience by exchanging turns, many of which were mere fragments from a structural point of view, was fascinating; the way in which this often delicate process was self-regulating, following unwritten rules and incorporating nonverbal actions into the making of meaning, contrasted sharply with the relative isolation of the written language, insulated largely from considerations of time and space.

Discourse analysis, then, set about devising suitable models and categories for description (e.g. Sinclair and Coulthard 1975). While using the experience of describing grammatical phenomena as far as was seen as relevant at that time, the researchers were much more aware of the differences than the similarities between informal conversation and tidy documents. The reception by grammarians of descriptions of discourse tended to emphasise the differences, and the upper boundary of grammar, the sentence, gained the status of a Dutch dyke, keeping out structures which had multiple origins.

After some decades, it is possible to return to these rather entrenched theoretical positions and reconsider them, in particular to look out for, and emphasise, aspects of structure which are shared regardless of the origin of a text. Conversation is an intriguing structure where participants simultaneously collaborate and compete, not unlike the structure of some games. They collaborate in many ways, for example by taking turns and by maintaining some continuity of topic. But on the other hand each participant has a personal agenda, something to achieve or avoid, often involving several conflicting aims; participants can be opportunistic as a situation develops, and much of their behaviour is unpredictable in all but the most general terms. They can superficially agree with each other but show merely by their choice of words that tensions remain under the surface; their agendas do not coincide.

In the early years of discourse study it was the competitive aspects of the structuration that were novel and commanded the attention of researchers; nothing of this kind had been observed in written language, and the simulations of speech in literary texts, dialogue in the novel and playscripts, did not show much similarity with real-time interaction. But in retrospect it can be seen that the co-operative aspect of conversation is just as interesting; the way in which coherence can be maintained and topics constantly updated while two or more quite independent individuals are expressing themselves apparently without restraint.

Linear Unit Grammar aims to redress the balance between the collaborative and the competitive by raising the profile of the collaborative aspects of discourse, the making of meaning through social interaction, using language. The competitive side comes under the organisational aspect of LUG, the "O" elements which, among other tasks, handle the real-time management of the conversation.

Chunking

It has been stated more than once that the approach to analysis presented in this book relies on a frequent observation about the way people cope with language in use. Fluent users of a language, asked to divide a text into small segments, perform the task with ease, and their responses are sufficiently similar for us to postulate that there are "natural units", often called *chunks*, discernible in text. Some of the major contributions to the study of chunks are discussed in Chapter 2. Here we will consider how chunks might fit into a theory of language.

First of all it is necessary to repeat that we treat *chunk* as a pre-theoretical term and therefore we do not try to define it. Everyone, we conclude from the extensive literature on the topic, acquires the ability to see a complex, multi-layered sentence as a string of short chunks. "Chunkability" manifests itself in several aspects of language structure because of the abundance of perceptible boundaries. In the phonology there are stress and tone patterns that have beginnings and endings, and pauses and junctures of various kinds; all of these are potential indicators of the possible dimensions and extent of chunks. Syntax envisages a text as divisible into a number of units, starting with the sentence as the largest unit, and the morpheme as the smallest; in between are found clauses, phrases and words. Clause and phrase boundaries are potentially chunk boundaries also, and punctuation marks in the written language. Lexical structures play a part too, with idiomatic phrases tending to stick together.

The perception of chunks, then, arises from a tension between the unfolding of a text word by word and the boundaries of the various analytic units, some of which coincide with each other. As each word is added to a chunk in progress and the chunk gets longer there is an increase in the likelihood of a boundary, and the coincidence of two or more of the various kinds of boundary mentioned above also increases the likelihood. We do not know enough about the various tensions and the interactions between them to make accurate predictions, but ultimately the cohesive aspects of the patterns are outweighed and overstretched, and — in the self-conscious mode that we are obliged to study—the speaker or reader assigns a text segment boundary and re-initiates the structure.

These considerations bring to mind a model from some years ago that fits the movements and tensions that we perceive in a user's handling of continuous text. In the seventies, the French mathematician René Thom elaborated his theory of *catastrophes*, where the combined effect of a number of factors causes a sudden change of state; the virtual certainty of the change of state is predicted, but it is not guaranteed to occur at any particular place. Thom's work became famous in explaining the "fight/flee" decisions of dogs under stress, and was used to predict events such as prison riots (Thom 1972).

The model is most appropriate to the prediction of boundaries; with each successive accretion to the discourse, each additional word, the data under active processing gets more and more complex and unwieldy, so pressure builds up towards packaging it and transferring it to a temporary storage facility, even if it is not completely coherent nor obviously complete. The process restarts with the word count at 1 again, and builds up to its next *catastrophe*.

If we list all the possible factors that may influence a chunk boundary, they are many and their interaction is too complicated to model in our present state of knowledge. But underneath the complexity lie simple, general and fundamental regularities which give us confidence in our analysis. The size of chunks in time intervals may well be linked to the regularity of breathing; we have as a kind of corroboration such evidence as a manuscript of Chaucer's *Canterbury Tales*, in which some word spaces are noticeably wider than others. The wider spaces occur fairly regularly and are thought to indicate places where pausing is appropriate, and thus make recitation of the poem easier.

The size of chunks which people feel comfortable with may be linked to the size of people's working memory. Since Miller's seminal paper on this subject (1956) it has been assumed that human beings can retain and process only a limited number of items at a time, and that as their attention shifts to something new, the previous contents of the working memory are gone. Some of the contents remain in long-term memory in a processed form, as a result of a normally subconscious process. This mental organisation fits the chunking model well; Miller's lower limit for the capacity of the short term memory is five items at a time, which is around the upper limit of words before a boundary is almost inevitable. The number of items held at one time varies somewhat, depending among other things on what works as one item — for example fixed phrases may constitute one item just like a word or part of a word — but the general principle holds.

While these links with physiology, through respiration, and psychology, through memory studies, do not constitute conclusive evidence for the reality of chunking, they are worth noting as consistent with the apparent strategies of interpretation of text that are studied in this volume. Phoneticians point out that all of the speech organs were originally developed for another function — the teeth, tongue, uvula, even the vocal cords themselves. So from an evolutionary perspective speech (and hence all language) is a secondary feature of the species, added onto an organism which was already extremely complex; compared with most bodily processes speech is remarkably superficial, merely an adaptation. A tendency towards chunking may have been part of the early adaptation of the species.

Linearity and alternation

The simplest code is a linear alternation of two symbols; this is the foundation of digital representations. There is only one possible relationship among symbols, which is that they are arranged in linear sequence, and the choice of each symbol is that it is either the same as the one before it or it is the other symbol.

Language text is essentially linear. Spoken language contains short sequences when more than one person speaks at once, but very soon one person emerges as "holding the floor" and is allowed to continue (see the section on linearity in Chapter 1).

The origin of our approach to analysis is to be found in Brazil's seminal work, *A Grammar of Speech*. Brazil (1995) replaces the central aim of received grammars, the description of sentences, with the aim of describing how people communicate using language, in his case spoken language. His contribution is summarised in Chapter 2.

Our hypothesis is that, at the initial level of analysis, language text can be interpreted as a simple linear binary code. The alternation is clearer and more frequent in informal spoken language, so we will start there. We assume that a contributor to a conversation has objectives, in that he or she wishes to update the state of common awareness with the other participants, and so we assume that some of the contributions will express suitable material for updating. But a conversation is a co-operative event with no single participant having the whole responsibility, so we assume that some of the contributions will deal with ensuring and maintaining a satisfactory level of co-operation, managing turn-taking and real-time factors, overcoming potential or actual obstacles, dealing with feedback from previous states of the conversation, coping with unexpected circumstances, simultaneous nonverbal activities, people coming or going, extraneous noise etc. This area also deals with the way in which contributions are organised with respect to each other, at least in the first instance; the explicitness or inexplicitness of the links between *topic increments* is seen as part of the negotiation of the increments themselves.

Hence we presume that from the start of a conversation, each participant is expecting to encounter a simple alternation of the two types of meaningful unit — the *organisation* unit and the topic increment. This is described in detail in Step Two (Chapter 6).

However, unlike a familiar binary code of alternating zeros and ones, the extent and boundaries of the units of the conversation code are not as clearly marked. Only the simplicity of the code and the tolerance of variation make it robust enough to remain as the basic structure.

The size of the two kinds of unit can differ a lot. Mostly the organisation units are rather short — just two or three words. In fast and informal conversation there is a frequent need for the deployment of these units to maintain the interaction, and if the topic increments are also quite short, as they often are, the discourse can be fairly evenly balanced between the two types, consisting of a frequent alternation between the two kinds of unit. In more formal or prepared kinds of discourse there is less need for organisation units of the kind that manage the interaction, since the structure of the interaction is to a larger extent predetermined by the prior acceptance of conventions. So in a lecture, for example, the participants tacitly agree not to make public verbal contributions throughout the event, thus obviating the need for mutual control of the turntaking. It does not, of course, remove the interactive dimension of the event, and audience reactions in the shape of nods and smiles and other gestures can shape a lecture importantly.

Writing characteristically does not take place in real time, nor in the presence of the readers, hence many of the organisation units that focus on interaction are not required, or required only occasionally. However, in writing greater prominence is given to the kind of text-oriented organisational units that handle the relations between increments, because the demand for text to be coherent is very strong.

Componence and position

We can demonstrate how linguistic units in text are recognised by referring to the two axes of language form, well-established in the literature since Saussure. These are the syntagmatic and the paradigmatic axes, conventionally represented horizontally and vertically respectively. A text forms along the syntagmatic axis and consists of a string of linguistic items chosen from what is available on the paradigmatic axis.

The syntagmatic axis thus provides *cotext*, an environment of other forms, and the paradigmatic axis provides *componence*, the shape of the particular item chosen. The way in which we recognise a linguistic unit depends on information gained from the intersection of these two factors. Occasionally the componence is unique, such as the pronoun *I* in English, the only single-letter word which is a capital letter, although it loses one of its distinctive features when it begins a sentence. Very occasionally the cotext is 100 percent decisive and the item can be confidently predicted, such as *kith and . . .* In the vast majority of cases we are dependent on information from both axes to make a positive identification.

In order to make use of information from both axes simultaneously, the interpreter must accept a degree of uncertainty. Decisions are almost always provisional, and rather than being confirmed by later events, the reality is that unless decisions are specifically shown to be inaccurate, the uncertainty just becomes gradually less relevant as the discourse unfolds. More immediate uncertainties have greater claim on the attention, and then they too gradually fade into obscurity.

The Linear Unit Grammar is designed to identify linguistic units called chunks. It is clear from the foregoing discussion that chunk identification is an approximate, not an exact, science, and we cannot expect high standards of interspeaker consistency. Far from it — this description, that aims to encompass all the subliminal analytic preferences of millions of individuals, will be quite different in character from the rigid architectures that we are familiar with. It will be extremely flexible, and will recognise the provisional nature of most of the assignments. It will not attempt to gather in one place all the relevant evidence concerning a stretch of text and make a decision that cannot be modified or even rescinded at another stage, but instead it will approximate towards the best fit between decisions and data at each stage.

LUG has thus been designed to be loose enough for all sorts of varieties of English to feel comfortable inside it; but as regards criteria for assignment it should be precise almost to the standard of being computable. Because a description is based on a series of decisions taken at different stages in an iterative process, each decision is simple and most can be taken by language users who do not have specialist training in linguistics. This stepped approach to analysis could make language descriptions more accessible to learners who have trouble with the abstractions of current presentations.

Traditionally, grammars have been written on the supposition that each user of a language has internalised exactly the same grammar — in the broad sense of grammar as a complete organised explanatory description of the language. This is extremely unlikely to be the case, but it has nevertheless been a characteristic assumption, even in dialectology, and it has been made explicit in the famous idealised speaker-hearer community of Chomsky (1965:3). Among real communities, it is more likely that users have internalised *approximately* the same grammar, with the approximations varying quite a lot in a widespread, much used language such as English. The way in which users deal with the places where their grammars do not exactly match is just as important as the way in which they handle the shared area of description, and an adequate theory will provide a systematic framework for the description of both the common ground and the gaps.

Prospection

A description of language structure is essentially a series of statements that limit the possibilities of linear combination in a text. If all combinations were possible, there would be no such thing as structure; in fact in most cases only a tiny proportion of the possible combinations ever occur. So structure reduces uncertainty, which is important when people's language varies from one individual to another, and when the text itself can sometimes be indeterminate.

Structure thus plays two important roles in the interpretation of texts. It helps in the identification of components, and it allows the reader or listener to *prospect* ahead and make informed guesses about what is likely to come. So instead of the listener hearing a burst of sound and then trying to work out what it means, the listener will be half-expecting one of a few options, and will only need to confirm which one it is. In these circumstances it is possible to interpret a sound wave which hardly contains enough information to signal its meaning. The more predictable a component is, the more risks a speaker can take with its pronunciation.

The prospective quality of structure also means that the text needs less of the listener's close attention; where the signals are merely confirmatory they are not likely to be problematic. So we may expect users of a language to be very sensitive to the structural possibilities at various places as a text unfolds. It is quite likely, also, that the frequency of phraseological patterns informs the prospections. So prospection is not an exact set of predictions in most cases, but a practical aid to quick and efficient interpretation.

Most conversations are collaborative and conform to expectations, and so give support to prospection as a powerful strategy; similarly most ordinary documents make use of the user's skill in prospection. Many precepts about style, such as the avoidance of cliché, entail the shared awareness of predictability in text, and many jokes exploit it. Some literary texts also exploit prospection, and many ironies depend on the contrast between the text that occurs and the one that would satisfy the prospections.

Completion

We have pointed out that language text is linear, and so far we have discussed the placement of provisional unit boundaries between chunks, which is the first step towards a non-linear view of the text; boundaries define chunks which, once identified, can be arranged in a non-linear relationship as well as a linear one.

The provisional boundaries that emerge from the chunking exercise express a variety of relationships that are set out in detail in Chapters 6, 7 and 8. But it is likely that speakers are aware of and sensitive to another boundary, of a hierarchical nature, which is of major importance in the interpretation of texts. To appreciate this we must consider the mechanism of prospection from a textual point of view rather than that of a reader or listener.

The reason that users of a language can prospect what linguistic choices may occur at a later point in the text is that the words and phrases that have occurred have induced a sense of semantic-structural incompleteness. The following fragment ends in a speaker change:

you're simply aware that you are having this experience of green not that you[1]

There is something missing; the text has set up an expectation that the speaker will provide an alternative to having an experience of green, but another speaker intervenes. On the other hand, this fragment does not prospect anything further:

you might get into a whole mess though[2]

However, after the interruption of a laugh, the speaker continues:

if you start like talking about all that stuff

The addressees understand the second part as an optional continuation of the first, not prospected but quite normal when it occurs. The first part, then, is *complete* as a potential unit of meaning, but not *finished* as an actual topic increment. This distinction helps us to model the way in which speakers and writers make use of prospection.

There is some connection between the Chomskyan distinction of "competence" and "performance" (1965: 4) and our categories of *complete* and *finished*. In both cases the first term refers to an abstract state when the properties of a structure are considered separately from any actual instance of it; the second term concerns the

---

[1]. This fragment is from the MICASE corpus, a philosophy seminar SEM475MX041. http://micase.umdl.umich.edu/m/micase/

[2]. MICASE seminar on composition SEM300MU100

details of an actual instance. But there are substantial differences in the way the categories of *complete* and *finished* are disposed.

The Chomskyan notion of "well-formedness" is relevant to both complete and finished structures, but our categories do not relate to a hypothetical grammar; instead they concern the likely perceptions of a participant in a conversation (or a reader) as the text unfolds. Unlike the notion of "well-formedness", conformity to received grammatical norms is a relatively minor criterion compared with whether the participant, at any point during an *emerging* utterance, is in a state of expectation of more information in order to complete the interpretation of the utterance up to that point. See *Inclusion and exclusion*, below, for some further points about well-formedness.

One origin of expectations is the semantic properties of individual words. This kind of expectation is set out very comprehensively in, for example, Harris (1982), who points out (ibid: 2) that the verb *entail* in English requires the presence of two other words such as *departure*, *termination* which in turn each require the presence of further words. This is a programmatic view of language, to which occurring text does not always conform. In text these "requirements" are just tendencies, and the strength of their prospective force depends on interaction with other factors. Harris also states that "simple nouns" such as *man*, *rock* do not depend on any other words for their occurrence, while in actual text their occurrence gives rise to further expectations, such as a preceding determiner and a verb.

The frequency of phraseological patterns is another origin of expectations, because prospection arises from experience, and so common patterns will be more securely expected than rare ones. There is an unlimited number of word combinations which, if they were to occur, would be deemed to be well-formed, but which do not lead to expectations in a user that they will occur. On the other hand, some freely-formed utterances are so predictable that speakers can finish each other's constructions.

The usual way in which a listening participant realises that a structure is finished is when a word or phrase occurs which cannot be interpreted as an extension of the emerging structure. It is not often remarked in language description that whereas the opening of structural units is often marked by an initialising item, the closing of them is rarely marked. Once complete, in the abstract sense, they can then simply be replaced by the start of another one.

The same simple mechanism applies whether the emerging unit is complete or not, and whether or not it is occasioned by speaker change. One way or another, participants become aware that utterances are finished because of the occurrence of an incompatible element. For example, here is the first example above with its immediate continuation:

> A: *you're simply aware that you are having this experience of green not that you*
> B: *in a perceptual case what this book's saying is that*

The first speaker is simply interrupted, and B makes no attempt at continuing the point. The first word, *in*, is unlikely to be compatible with the previous phrasing, and indeed it appears that the word introduces a completely different aspect of the topic.

The prospections, while not capable of being itemised, are strong and detailed. We can imagine an addressee in a conversation listening to successive chunks and noting the structure, and in particular whether or not a structure is complete; if it is incomplete then the prospection is for something to complete it; if it is complete then the prospection is that the next unit will either be an extension that will fit in with the emerging structure, or an incompatible element, which will indicate that the previous structure is finished and a new one is emerging.

In traditional grammars of the written language the mark of "finishedness" was the sentence boundary. "Sentence" is only a valid category in continuous written prose, and is thus not general enough to be an important descriptive category from the theoretical perspective of LUG.

Matching

As well as being alert to the prospective nature of language text, users are also prepared to encounter successive stretches of text that are very similar to each other. This phenomenon, called *matching*, offers an alternative to the structural interpretations that we have featured so far.

> *the key area isn't a key area it starts on . . . it starts somewhere, and goes somewhere,*
> *. . . violin concertos in which the solos, precisely the solos did the modulating*[3].

These are examples of the everyday use of matching, here used in a lecture to highlight important points. The first example contains two: an article followed by *key area*, looks like a contradiction but it is a familiar rhetorical tactic; then the word *somewhere* is repeated, forming a frame within which *starts* contrasts with *goes*. In the second example the repeated *the solos* draw attention to themselves and also to the word *precisely*, which is added. Clearly in order to understand these, the listeners have to be aware of the repetitions and the changes; it is not appropriate to analyse these examples as a succession of words related only to the words immediately round about.

---

3. Both instances from MICASE seminar on music LES420MG134

A match is the interpretation of a segment of speech or writing as the recurrence of a similar segment in fairly close proximity; its interpretation differs somewhat between speech and writing, so we will first, and mainly, consider the spoken medium. Some circumstance of the immediate situation has led the speaker to reformulate a segment, but in essentially the same terms.

Matches need not be identical — the requirement is merely that they are interpreted as inescapably associated with a previous stretch of text. If identical their purpose may be to control the real-time aspects of the conversation — to give speakers time to think, for example, or to react to the perception of a challenge to their utterance, whether someone is trying to take over the speaker role, or is registering an objection to the line of argument, or is losing interest in the utterance. Alternatively, an identical repeat may occur if the speaker is distracted and is recovering the thread of his/her argument. In general, exact repeats arise from the short-term, existential requirements of making an effective contribution to the discourse, and do not have implications beyond the moment of their occurrence.

If matches are slightly different, but still easily interpreted as matches, then their normal purpose is to rephrase, in a more convenient way, something that the speaker wants to say. While in the process of uttering something, the speaker appreciates that there is another way of expressing it, or something similar in the particular circumstances, and starts again. Perhaps the perception is that the opportunities in the lexical grammar are not convenient for the phrasing that is under way, and a better formulation is attempted. There are other functions, of course — for example on restarting after an interruption, a speaker may summarise the previous position with a similar but less elaborate phrasing. Most of the quasi-repeats have mainly existential significance, but some may signal difficulties in expression, or difficulties in putting over a point of view or trying to formulate an emerging thought. These are pragmatic meanings that may need to be retained as part of the record of experience.

Matches need not be complete units. If incomplete they can be interrupted either by the speaker or by some external event, whether part of the discourse or not. Of the first variety, one common type is occasioned by the speaker reconsidering how to put some matter; there is not a great deal of difference between complete and incomplete matches by the same speaker. In the case of external interruptions, a return to the phraseology that was interrupted is a fairly safe way of maintaining coherence despite the interruption.

Matches can be rhetorical, structural or subliminal. Rhetorical matches are drawn to the attention of the participants, are often memorable, as in some kinds of oratory. They are foregrounded, and can be important elements in the rhetorical architecture of a discourse, whether rehearsed or impromptu. Structural matches occur when the reader/listener interprets a match as forming a stable background to two or more items which are then compared or contrasted. This occurs, for example, in expository language like lectures (Mauranen forthcoming b) and in dictionary definitions. Subliminal matches are those that the participants are largely unaware of; typically, subliminal matches are not remembered with any accuracy, and if a conversational fragment is reported to a third party, they are normally omitted.

In the written language there are only rhetorical and structural matches; subliminal ones are removed in the editing process. Many literary figures depend on matching (Sinclair forthcoming), and ordinary effective writing makes frequent use of small-scale matches, e.g.

> *But more important, he would see the great damage his laws are doing to the institutions we have inherited—to the constitution, to the tradition of parliamentary sovereignty, to the independence of the judiciary, to individual rights and to the delicate relationship between the individual and the state.*[4]

Collaborative discourse

Received notions of discourse are not as ancient as those of grammar, but they are fairly generally accepted: there are at least two participants, whose behaviour is a tension between co-operation and competition. At the beginning of this chapter it was pointed out that participants have separate, and almost certainly differing, agendas, but in order to fulfil their goals they must work carefully with other participants in maintaining their own credibility and the attention of the other participants. A conversation is similar in many respects to a game of alternating turns like tennis, where co-operation (i.e.observing the rules) is in tension with competition (creating conditions when points accrue to the player).

Transcriptions of spoken interaction tend to emphasise the co-operative/competitive tension of discourse; tags are interpolated to indicate change of speaker, and attempts (not always successful) to identify the speaker in order to relate a turn to previous and subsequent turns. Most transcriptions are set out like playscripts, where the turntaking is the most obvious structural device.

However, as was argued earlier, we can view a conversation from another perspective, that reduces the emphasis on participants and turntaking; Linear Unit Grammar attempts to do this, and here we argue a theoretical perspective which supports the analysis.

---

4. Henry Porter in The Observer 5.7.06

From a *purely textual* perspective there are always and only just two participants in a discourse. They are called *I* and *you*, and they are the only definite points where a text relates to the world outside. We observe — as a separate matter — that individuals take up these participant roles from time to time, but individuals are not, formally speaking, discourse participants; they can equally be seen as transient attributes of the *I* or *you* roles. The use of proper names in a conversation indicates intermittently which individual occupies one of the roles at a particular moment, but the same person can of course be addressed or referred to in a dozen different styles in a single conversation.

A communicative act entails an originator and a recipient; if there were no originator it would not exist, and the originator makes the assumption of a recipient or the act would be would be merely an expressive act, not a communicative one. These two participant roles are the only ones that recur regularly enough to be recognised in a general description. Names and titles are transitory. So if we consider a transcript of a conversation involving five people, some or all of those five from time to time take up the role of speaker or the role of addressee; but the tape shows only *I* and *you*. The only common variant is that *we* can occasionally be used if the speaker/writer is acting as spokesperson for a group.

The first of the transcripts in our small collection is necessarily of this kind; there is no indication of speaker change. While it becomes tricky to reconstruct in places exactly who said what, the topic increments emerge as readily as from a transcript in which each turn is carefully picked out and associated with a speaker.

The idea that a text recognises two and only two participants is one that can be teased out much more than the needs of this book determine; it looks like a universally valid statement, and it has profound implications for the study of cohesion and anaphora in general. It also plays a central role in semantic theory, in the relations between a text and the world. We are so accustomed to viewing language interaction from a human perspective, as a major component of our social lives, that it is refreshingly different to consider it from a strictly textual perspective.

Abstract grammars

It is pointed out frequently in this book that abstract grammars are only marginally relevant to the kind of structures that are the focus of Linear Unit Grammar. Abstract grammars are those that do not depend on the actual occurrence of any piece of language, and do not engage with the linear nature of text and do not attempt a methodical description of what actually occurs. Equally distant are more data-sensitive grammars of the normative kind that describe the approved language behaviour of highly-trained writers, and all the grammars that lie in between these extremes.

Our position is not in the least hostile to any of the received grammars, whether abstract or data-sensitive. It is perfectly reasonable to accept everything in this book and simultaneously believe that each speaker of a language has a mental picture of it which corresponds, roughly or precisely, to the claims that are made in the abstract grammar. It is not unreasonable to suppose that a received grammar which describes the approved patterns of written documents is a fairly similar construct to people's internal grammar, and not just a matter of social conformity. No counter-argument to these positions is mounted here. We are obliged to point out that these existing traditions of grammar are not able to make a satisfactory description of the material we present, all of which is recognisable and intelligible current English. The grammars are clearly not designed in such a way as to tackle the linearity of text, which, if not the starting point, has to be engaged at some point. They make no attempt to explain how speakers construct conversations jointly, nor how target readers influence the construction of documents. A few decades ago the linguistic study of discourse opened up new possibilities that we have taken advantage of here, but they stress the interactive, dialogic quality of the text rather than what is actually constructed — the "process" rather than the "product", to recall notions of thirty years ago.

Linear Unit Grammar is thus not a competitor with established grammars, but a complement to them; at the end of a LUG description the text should be available for input into an established grammar. Most of the relevant meaning-bearing patterns should be exposed. However, the experience of LUG description opens up an alternative route to a comprehensive description, one that is only outlined in this book. For the kind of iterative cycle of description that we have adopted can be continued, and the steps from linear to a more hierarchical structure can be made explicit using extensions of the techniques that are used in LUG. There are many potential advantages to continuing the description in this way and offering ultimately a grammar which is not limited in its coverage of the syntactic and lexical structures of the language, and which can then be evaluated against the magnificent body of structural description that already exists.

So, while LUG is initially offered as a complement to conventional grammar, covering an area that is not normally covered and a range of texts which is normally ignored, there is room for its further development. The one-pass, single-cycle hierarchical grammar has evolved over centuries and is efficient and good at its job; however, this job is no longer at the centre of linguistic priorities, and a complement such as LUG will shore up the reputation of conventional grammars for a little while longer.

Inclusion and exclusion

The main practical use of a grammar is to show by analysis how a stretch of text relates to the meaning that is acquired in the act of reading it or listening to it. That is the orientation of this book. However, an inescapable consequence of constructing a grammar is that it can be used to determine which stretches of text follow precisely its specifications, and which do not.

Formal and computational grammarians are well aware that this is a major issue; no artificial cap can be placed on human creativity, inventiveness and opportunism, and so no grammar is ever likely to anticipate every phraseological detail. The question is not whether unanticipated stretches occur, nor even how common they are, but what the grammar does about them. Here there are differences in approach that reflect both practical priorities and the theories that lie behind them.

On the one hand there is prescriptivism, which is sometimes taken to excess but which has many roles to play in areas such as language learning and literary explication. The grammatical description for such activities must be rigorous and the limits as clear as possible. On the other hand there are flexible grammars, like Linear Unit Grammar, which are designed to accommodate text rather than exclude it. In between is the theoretical study of "well-formedness", which seeks to specify the kind of grammatical principles which can be postulated to have correlates in the human brain, and which ultimately specify all possible sentences in all possible languages.

Each of these types of language study requires a grammar with different attributes. Linear Unit Grammar seeks to find a way of assigning meaning to stretches of text; rather than exclude a stretch on the grounds that ultimately it does not fit a set of predetermined specifications, LUG initially accepts it. Passing it through the steps of analysis, LUG gathers structural information — about its chunking, its O and M units, the LUMs that can be constructed from the textual evidence, the modifications to its linearity that bring out its coherence, etc. This information might not be complete in every case, but unusual stretches are not just abandoned. In the case of the *Gazetteer* text, the density and systematic nature of the unusual expressions suggests that a specific *local grammar* should be compiled — that is to say, the grammar is extended to cope with highly specialised texts. A local grammar mirrors the prescriptive end of the spectrum of grammars by specifying entry conditions so that it will only be used in appropriate circumstances.

Despite their different uses, the different kinds of grammar share a lot of information about the language, and so they can be seen as a number of routes which converge on a core of shared information. LUG offers a clear converging route, one which starts with text and accepts it as it is. One of David Brazil's favourite expressions for text was "used language" — language that had been authenticated by its participation in communication, in the incrementation of shared experience. Linear Unit Grammar seeks to explain how this incrementation is achieved, using a series of steps that gradually align the used language with the more abstract blueprints that other grammars deal with.

Summary conclusion

The argument of this chapter can be summarised in a few hypotheses that appear below. Primarily the chapter presents an account of the way in which a description of text can first relax the strict linearity of text, and then postulate new groupings of a potentially hierarchical nature. The argument combines observations about the nature of text and suggestions about the strategies that people use in interpreting text.

The hypotheses are consistent with other independent observations in this field, such as the studies of chunking that have been carried out, the statements about the dependencies of words on each other, as regards occurrence, and aspects of the structure of text which imply certain strategies. The resultant analysis is compatible with the categories of received grammar, but does not depend on them for its validity.

- Language text can readily be divided into small segments of a few words in length, which are coherent with respect to the meaning of the text.
- The primary structure of text is a linear alternation of units of organisation of the discourse and units of incrementation of the topic.
- The structure of text is indicated by a combination of the position of linguistic units with respect to each other, and their componence.
- The structure of a text makes possible the prospection of what may follow a unit which is in process of realisation.
- Language users prospect the completion of utterances.
- Language users are aware of matches and able to interpret them
- From a textual perspective, there are two and only two participants in a discourse, and their names are *I* and *you*.

CHAPTER 12

Looking ahead

The work reported in this book was undertaken in a general spirit of enquiry, and without any applications in mind. As a descriptive system took shape it gave rise to speculations about its utility value, first in reconciling spoken and written texts, which we built into the research, particularly in Chapter 10. Then we saw possibilities in emphasising the linear and syntagmatic side of grammars, to act as a small counterbalance to the paradigmatic grammars that are found in linguistics generally. This far our initiative was in text description pure and simple, but when we reached a point where we thought regular grammars could take over, we realised that their paradigmatic orientation would constitute a substantial deviation from the kind of description that we had embarked on. So we took one further step towards a more comprehensive syntagmatic grammar. To go any further would have altered the main thrust of our argument; scholars can accept and work with the first five steps of LUG and align LUG output with the input protocols of another grammar of their choice.

The decision to separate O and M units at an early stage, followed by the observation that O units were severely constricted in their structural options, led to optimism that some steps in automation could be considered, and the glimpse that this afforded into the information extraction and text mining of the future spurred us on. While our present analysis involves careful subjective judgement, many aspects of the design of the system should lend themselves to replication in an automaton, and attempts to automate stages or components of Linear Unit Grammar are likely to shed a lot of light on the process of deriving meaning from texts.

At the same time we were becoming aware that our description was more direct and accessible to non-experts than its predecessors. It does not require initial investment in the highly abstract categories of a top-down grammar nor the great complexity of a single-cycle grammar, and yet it is possible to cover a great amount of the grammar of English, as well as integrating many structural features which, while recognised in discourse analysis, had not made the transition into the grammar of phrases and clauses.

These matters are discussed below under the heading of *Prospects for Linear Unit Grammar*. At the same time it gradually became clear that the simplicity and accessibility of the Grammar could turn out to be valuable in several applications, particularly those in which the participants needed occasionally to have an analysis of the text they were working with, but were not expert descriptive linguists and had no intention of becoming any more expert than was required for their jobs. This could cover a large area of activity, including language teaching and learning, and in many parts of the language industries, particularly in translation. So we have introduced this aspect of application and set out a few possibilities later on in this chapter, under the heading *Applications of Linear Unit Grammar*.

Prospects for Linear Unit Grammar

Alignment with other grammars

For input to regular grammars the analysed version, with boundaries showing and OT items tagged, will give the grammars a head start. We would expect a close alignment of unit boundaries between Linear Unit Grammar and ordinary grammars. Former MS elements, for example, should map precisely onto various constructions of the "qualifier" variety; LUM (linear unit of meaning) boundaries between contiguous M elements should map onto coherent segments of clauses or phrases. Within a LUM the jobs of determining the syntactic relations, parts of speech etc. are made easier because of the provisional boundaries, the PUBs, that were assigned during the analysis.

As an example of this, we note that PUBs often separate prepositional phrases from the preceding text, thus distinguishing them from the same words counting as adverbs. There are two places, for example, in Step 5 (7c), where the prepositions *about* and *for* are firmly linked to their following noun phrases and separated from the structures preceding them. While a human interpreter is unlikely to find it perplexing to make these decisions, a computer must entertain the possibility, unless told otherwise, that the two words are adverbs, and that the following noun phrases initiate a new structure.

> *it was an article/I read/**about** a famous Estonian*
> *the citizenship law/**for** the Russians*

Let us compare these with three prepositions in Step 5 (6b):

> *to look **at**/tax policy/<u>as well as</u>/a number **of**/internal reviews/**into** the party's structure*

The OT item is underlined, and the slashes indicate PUBs. The third preposition, *into*, opens an MS chunk like *about* and *for* above, but the other two are more left-oriented; *look at* is a phrasal verb, therefore *at* is drawn towards *look*, while *of* is normally more closely associated with the noun in front of it rather than the one that follows (Sinclair 1991; Krishnamurthy ed. 2004: 157). This phrase in particular, *a number of*, is a common three-word phrase in English, well known to any fluent speaker.

In such cases of mismatch between the chunking of a particular text and the provisions of a general grammar, the analyst is alerted to the likelihood that the prepositions are components of lexical structures that take precedence over grammatical ones. The output from LUG, then, contains a considerable amount of information useful for analysis, and all of it is compatible with conventional categories. In particular the chunks divide text into quite small segments, within which the syntactic relations may be determined without influence from the outside; the analytic process can thus be staged. The full benefit of this will not be seen until a comprehensive "hybrid" parser is developed, a parser which relates syntactic constraints to the particular phraseology of a text at a certain point.

The Linear Unit Grammar can thus be seen, and used, as a novel kind of shallow or partial parser; one with a life of its own, which does not strive to mesh precisely with established general grammars, but which covers a substantial proportion of the analysis that those grammars require as well as covering an area into which they do not penetrate. LUG does not rely for its credibility on these grammars, but on its fidelity to the data and to the accuracy and utility of its own theoretical stance. Where its conclusions are similar to the familiar ones of established grammar, that is because the two systems are applied to similar data, and is probably influenced by the fact that the authors of this book ultimately belong to the same intellectual tradition as the present and previous influential grammarians.

There are some substantial differences, however; for example we separate OTs from their surroundings at an early stage, and they remain separate. At Step 2 we found that they are closer in function to OI than to M units, and, componentially, their construction seems to involve, like OI, fewer open-choice decisions. Having identified them thus early, we see no need to return them inside clauses by imposing one particular view of the clause on them, where there are other views of the clause of which one fits the case precisely (see Chapter 1, Clause boundaries). This position is incompatible with a model which requires, a priori, that every constituent unit of a sentence is a clause, but in analytic practice these two positions are fairly easy to reconcile.

LUG output can be presented in a variety of formats; as we have seen, one is in plain text format with reasonable punctuation and topic flow, so that it can be read with relative ease by anyone who can read ordinary printed text. The same text can be presented with as much of the analysis as possible included, either through tagging, or special layout conventions, or notes, or some combination of these. With the extra information in this format, LUG output can be seen as contributing to a range of applications in information science.

Another option open to us is to continue to develop LUG in its own terms, following the style of description that it has opened up for us. There are in existence many large and prestigious descriptions of English, and it was never our intention to invade their territory. However, they are of quite a different character to LUG, and treat data differently; the integration of LUG output with such grammars, while easy enough to achieve, is a radical change of direction; a sudden switch to a heavily hierarchical model, likely to obscure some of the points uncovered by LUG.

Syntagmatic relations

On the other hand it is relatively straightforward to take one further step in analysis, pursuing the same strategy as before — settling on a simple choice which can be applied to the relationship between items in a linear string, and which contributes to the elucidation of the way in which form creates meaning. It will still not lead to an exhaustive description, but will indicate possible ways forward that are largely independent of established grammars.

The starting point is to be found in Bloomfield (1933: 194 ff.). There we find the terms *endocentric* and *exocentric*, which we propose to adapt and adopt for our analysis. Nida (1960: ix–lviii) uses the same terms in similar ways. But Bloomfield's definitions are not suitable for our purposes, even though we want to use the terms to indicate very similar linguistic items. For Bloomfield an exocentric construction is one where a construction made of two or more "immediate constituents" does not belong to any of the recognised form-classes. So in his example, *John ran* is exocentric; on the other hand, *poor John* is an endocentric construction because "the forms *John* and *poor John* have, on the whole, the same functions". The argument requires us to accept that *poor* and *John* belong to the same general form-class, and to accept that for some reason there should not be established a form-class for subject-predicate constructions despite their frequency.

This kind of definition is not appropriate today, but its general import remains relevant — we are aware of a sort of "like/unlike" distinction in the groupings of words in text. For our version of it we begin by establishing a category that is fundamental to this study, arising as it does from our first differentiation of chunks.

First, we use Step 2 to pick out the O elements and deal with them separately; they are not appropriately handled by normal grammatical apparatus of the kind that Bloomfield and other grammarians set up; the structural options available to them are strictly limited, and the vast majority of the realisations of both OI and OT are listable in a finite list with very few variable constituents. In terms of a continuum between the *open-choice* and *idiom* principle they tend to follow the idiom principle (Sinclair 1991); hence the simplest grammar for them will be a small *local grammar* (Barnbrook and Sinclair 2001). We do not pursue the classification of O-elements any further.

The remainder of this section deals only with M elements. The choice at each word boundary in an M element is between endocentric and exocentric. Note that we maintain the focus on the boundary and do not ask what is inside apart from the words on either side of the space. This avoids problematic decisions about which words are "like" each other, and retains a largely linear view of the text.

We ask at each boundary what kind of relationship holds between the words on either side.

(a) do the words combine to make a single *textual object*, or
(b) do the words remain separate and therefore contribute towards the expression of a *textual incident*?

Textual objects include the main traditional word classes, nouns, adjectives, verbs and adverbs, either on their own or as heads of phrases; a textual object is a construct that must combine with another in order to be deployed in a communicative act. It can act as a reference point, a construction that draws attention to itself, but does not of itself increment the virtual world of shared experience (but see below). The main relationship among the words that make up a textual object is modification, and the relation that holds among members of a textual object is the endocentric relation.

A textual incident, on the other hand, requires at least two separate objects to be combined, and expresses relations like those of subject/predicate, verb/object, preposition/noun phrase. The expression of a textual incident updates the virtual world and changes it. The relation that holds among components of a textual incident is the exocentric relation.

The distinguishing feature of an endocentric relation is that the items that constitute the relationship make a meaningful construction because of their *combinability* into a single entity, a textual object. The distinguishing feature of an exocentric relation is that the items that constitute the relationship make a meaningful construction by maintaining their *separateness*, and remaining two distinct entities, although a single construction.

Each of these brief descriptions requires to be given a lot more detail; here we will attempt only to avoid confusions. It is necessary to explain why a single, isolated textual object can be interpreted as updating shared experience, as making a statement, and therefore fulfilling the same communicative function as a textual incident. There seems to be a paradox here — the definition of a textual object precludes a function which is widespread in notices, titles, labels and many other items in daily use. Single word examples include "private", "closed", "Ladies", "lift". Multi-word textual objects are also common; a book title, for example, or the first three words of this sentence after the semicolon. Plenty of instances can be found to validate this apparent contradiction of the definition of a textual object — indeed it seems that we frequently regard endocentric structures as if they fulfilled the requirements of textual incidents.

A textual incident requires us to identify two separate elements. If only one is a textual object, then the other must be *con*textual, and must of course be identified. A book title, for example, can combine with the book itself; the title normally occupies the most prominent position on the front of the book and is often repeated on the spine. The act of expressing a title is a textual incident.

In the passage referred to above, the three words *a book title*, give us a clear instance of a noun phrase that appears to be the entire textual expression of a textual incident, despite its endocentric construction. The other component arises from the cotext, because the previous sentence prospects that it will be followed by a sentence which will contain an exemplar of the passage "a single, isolated textual object [which] can be interpreted as updating shared experience, as making a statement". The OT in the sentence, *for example*, is a confirmation of this relationship since it points out that both *a book title* and *the first three words of this sentence* are exemplars.

So we conclude that a textual object can act as a component of a textual incident in one of two ways — it can combine with another TO or a TI in an exocentric relationship, or it can combine with an observable feature of the context of situation, something that can be identified and cited if necessary. J. R. Firth's often quoted list of the components of a context of situation (1957: 182) includes "the relevant objects", and one criterion of relevance is surely combination with a TO to make the equivalent of a TI, and thus a potentially complete topic increment. Returning to basics, a TI must relate together in a coherent fashion at least two independently meaningful items. The resolution of the apparent paradox mentioned above is that a relevant contextual object may be adduced as one of the meaningful items.

Earlier grammars used categories like "ellipsis" or "words understood" to explain this kind of phenomenon, but now that many linguists respect the actual wordings of corpora, and are committed to describing the text and not some rewritten version of it, notions that there are some words missing or that the text cannot be understood as it stands are no longer tenable. As the Gazetteer text shows, text need not always be as explicit as it is in the norms of written language; it may not be analysable into subjects and objects, but it is perfectly intelligible.

Topic increment

We call the LUMs *topic increments* because they update the virtual world of shared experience of the participants in a discourse (or that of readers of written documents). With each member of our society with whom we are on speaking terms we share a virtual world that includes all our previous joint experience, verbal and nonverbal. Most of this may be subliminal most of the time, surfacing as broad emotional reactions, feelings of pleasure or concern, adjustment of formality levels, etc.; but we may be vividly aware of some past experiences which guide the strategies used in the present one. When there is more than one participant, the virtual worlds overlap according to memories, conscious or not, of collective and separate shared experience. The constant implicit and explicit reference to these virtual worlds gives a distinctive quality to the conversation or document.

J. R. Firth, in an unpublished lecture given in Edinburgh in 1959, pointed out this out with reference to drama, instancing *The Merchant of Venice* as his text. He showed that most of the characters in that play interacted within small peer groups, giving them little opportunity to show the range of their shared experience; as a result they appear to be two-dimensional, cardboard characters. Only Shylock interacts with everyone, with his daughter, with fellow merchants, with lawyers and judges, with other Jews. We thus get many perspectives in Shylock's aggregate of virtual worlds, and he is the dominant personality in the play. Firth is claiming that a dramatist can control our assessments of characters not only by the things they say and do, but also by their conversational groupings, who they meet and who they talk to.

Analysis

Here is an example of the next stage of LUG analysis, explained above; the application of the basic, binary, linear distinction between *endocentric* and *exocentric* relations. The passage comes from the Lexis text, a little later in the conversation than the extract chosen to illustrate the previous steps in analysis.

> *I wondered what happens when you go from one island to the other no the train goes on the ferry oh I see yes*

The text is first chunked (Step 1) into:

I wondered
what happens
when you go
from one island
to the other
no
the train goes
on the ferry
oh
I see
yes

That is to say, each line end indicates the placement of a Provisional Unit Boundary. As we have seen, these breaks are not obligatory, and there are other plausible readings, e.g.

> *I wondered what happens/when you go/from one island/to the other/no/the train/ goes on the ferry/oh I see/yes*

However, the breaks are not arbitrary either, and the following is most unlikely, and would probably be dismissed as perverse by fluent users:

> **I wondered what/happens when you/go from one/island to the/other no the/train goes on the/ferry oh I/see yes*

Step 2 will pick out *no* and *oh I see yes* as concerned with the interaction (including changes of speaker); these are classed as OI elements and do not take part in the present process. Step 3 does not apply in this example.

Step 4 classifies the M elements:

I wondered	M–
what happens	+M–
when you go	+M–
from one island	+M–
to the other	+M
the train goes	M–
on the ferry	+M

Step 5 concatenates the elements into two LUMs:

> 1. *I wondered/what happens/when you go/from one island/to the other*
> 2. *the train goes/on the ferry*

We retain the slashes as reminders of chunk boundaries.

The next step requires a decision to be taken at each word break between endocentric and exocentric; at first within chunks:

Word	Relation	Word	Relation	Word
		I	exocentric	*wondered*
		what	exocentric	*happens*
when	exocentric	*you*	exocentric	*go*
from	exocentric	*one*	endocentric	*island*
to	exocentric	*the*	endocentric	*other*
the	endocentric	*train*	exocentric	*goes*
on	exocentric	*the*	endocentric	*ferry*

Then we add the relations at the chunk boundaries:

Word	Relation	Word	Relation	Word	PUBs
		I	exocentric	*wondered*	exocentric
		what	exocentric	*happens*	exocentric
when	exocentric	*you*	exocentric	*go*	exocentric
from	exocentric	*one*	endocentric	*island*	exocentric
to	exocentric	*the*	endocentric	*other*	LUM end
the	endocentric	*train*	exocentric	*goes*	exocentric
on	exocentric	*the*	endocentric	*ferry*	LUM end

This can be summarised by bracketing the endocentric constructions together and putting curly brackets round LUMs:

{*I wondered*/*what happens*/*when you go*/*from* [*one island*]/*to* [*the other*]}
{[*the train*] *goes*/*on* [*the ferry*]}

We now have a kind of unlabelled bracketing; endocentric constructions occur within exocentric ones, and those occur within LUMs, so there is the beginnings of a hierarchy present. What is not resolved is the relative status of successive exocentric units. For example, a conventional grammar would require the three prepositional phrases to be incorporated within the previous constructions to make clauses. This is easy to do, but in the present state of our analysis it is unmotivated. If we view a text not as a lump in process of construction, but as an evolving state, then *when you go* prospects and introduces the following phrases but has no further stake in them. *From one island* prospects and introduces *to the other* but again is not required again in the LUM. The same relationship characterises the first two chunks, and the passage as a whole shows a distinctly Markovian character, in that each successive chunk performs its function and then, from a structural point of view, can be discarded. True, there is concord maintained in the verb tenses, but that is also true across the LUM boundary, and is clearly a property of the discourse rather than of a LUM or chunk.

At this point, then, most of the structural features are determined, and the presentation is largely a matter of choice on the part of the analyst. A further stage can add traditional clause boundaries, and the elements of clause structure can be identified. In this particular passage, the verbs (*wondered, happens, go, goes*) are fairly clearly indicated morphologically and the pronouns and *when* are unique forms; *what* is a slippery word in English as a whole, but not here, where the boundaries compel it to act as subject.

This example seems rather straightforward. Let us explore another one, one of a more balanced interaction, the conversation from the HKCSE corpus, which is fully analysed in Chapter 10.

First we remove the OI and MF segments, then put together pairs of M– and +M, then merge the MR element with preceding formulations. We are left with:

{[deep-fried pork chop]}/
{and then with [the butter]}/
{it [must be] [a kind of Japanese mushroom]}/
{[the long thin white one] }/
{[the other one] is [the rice]}/*
{it's [the roast beefs]}

Each LUM is on a new line, the OT is underlined and the bracketing is as before. Those PUBs that have survived the deletions and combinations follow the new LUM boundaries very closely. The asterisk denotes the presence of a note; the relationship of the last LUM to the preceding text needs some explanation, which is dealt with in the descriptive notes that accompany the edited text where necessary (as explained in Step 5).

Again this analysis comes close to what would be expected of any competent grammar of English. Note that *must be* shows an endocentric relationship, and the phrase thus is a textual object. *Of* does not break the endocentricity of the noun phrase in the third LUM.

There could be an issue with *deep-fried* in the first LUM. We interpret this as a modifying participle and so endocentric on both sides; however the form is nearly identical to that of a past tense verb, and the hyphen cannot be guaranteed in modern orthography. Although there is little room for doubt in this instance, some diagnostic is necessary to clarify words of this kind, and the extra information supplied by the various boundaries and their syntactic relationships will make the task simpler and more reliable.

Summary of Linear Unit Grammar

In the following paragraphs the categories and options of the grammar are set out in a regimented format, with the choices reduced to binaries.

We begin with the input, which is, in principle, any text in English that is expressed in a linear alphanumeric stream. The output is an analysed version of the text, along with notes on real-time matters where appropriate.

The output is marked up as a sequence of *textual incidents,* interspersed with *textual organisers* (OTs). Textual incidents are units of meaning (LUMs) which have internal exocentric relations.

The components of a textual incident include other textual incidents of a minor nature, *textual objects* and textual organisers. Textual objects are LUMs which have internal endocentric relations.

A linear unit of meaning (LUM) consists of a core M element and any dependent Ms. Dependent Ms are +M, M−, +M−, MS, MR and MA. O and M units are made up of words.

There are also intermediate units, which are MF (message fragment) and OI (interaction organiser). These do not appear in the output, but they may give rise to accompanying notes.

The choices between structural elements can be represented as an orderly series of binary choices. The first choice is the **orientation**:

1. Action-oriented: O
2. Message-oriented: M

The next choice for O elements is their **focus**:

1.1 Situation-focused: OI
1.2 Text-focused: OT

There is no further classification of O elements proposed at present, though they perform a wide variety of discourse roles. More extended versions of this grammar could include a classification of OIs, which would begin to integrate discourse and grammar.

M choices are more complex. First there is the **status** of the M element:

2.1 Core status: M
2.2 Qualified status: all other Ms

There is no further subdivision of core M proposed at this stage. It will be found that Ms are readily analysed by conventional grammars, and that they may make such small demands on a grammar that a local grammar could be adequate. If so there would be no need to call on the power of a general grammar.

Qualified M breaks down into *linear expectations*:

2.2.1 Prospecting (a following M):   M−, MF, MA
2.2.2 Additional: +M, MS

Prospecting Ms divide according to *substantialness* into:

2.2.1.1 Substantial: MA, M−
2.2.1.2 Insubstantial: MF

Substantialness involves a judgement as to whether a sufficient amount of text has been uttered to make it necessary to retain it as part of a topic increment. As we have pointed out, many chunks that we classify as MF are so brief and inconclusive that they are called M because an "OF" is an unlikely event.

Then Substantial Ms divide on the issue of *interpenetration*:

2.2.1.2.1 Overlapping: MA
2.2.1.2.2 Separate: M–

Returning to 2.2.2. Additional Ms also divide according to *linear expectations*:

2.2.2.1 prospected: +M
2.2.2.2 unexpected: MS, MR.

The Unexpected Ms are again differentiated by *interpenetration*:

2.2.2.2.1 Overlapping   MR
2.2.2.2.2 Separate   MS

The remaining M elements are:
+M–, which is a combination of 2.2.1.1 "qualified prospecting substantial separate" and 2.2.2.1 "qualified additional prospected"
+MF, which is a combination of 2.2.1.2 "qualified prospecting insubstantial" and 2.2.2.1 "qualified additional prospected"
MS–, which is a combination of 2.2.1.1 "qualified prospecting substantial separate" and 2.2.2.2.2 "qualified additional unexpected separate"

Note that while the grammar is set out like a system network (Halliday 1985), the choices are mainly syntagmatic rather than paradigmatic. Choices such as qualified, prospecting, overlapping deal with the sequence of events in the text and the inter-relations of the structural elements, rather than with the usual kind of paradigmatic choices. The initial pair of choices, O and M, can hardly be presented as paradigmatic alternatives, nor the distinction between OI and OT. These choices, and our interpretations of them, are largely determined by the state of the text at the time of choice; in the spoken language by the real-time speech situation and in the written language by the emerging architecture of the passage.

Applications of Linear Unit Grammar

Language and information science

In Step 5 of our analysis (Chapter 9) we showed how the various texts we used could be output as word sequences which expressed the incremental import of the original with reasonable accuracy, and which also carried indications of the kinds of structures that established grammars can accept as input.

The work presented in this book should not, however, be judged by the relative success or failure of this kind of output. The final output stage of Step 5 has been arranged to look reasonably like continuous prose in order to offer a familiar frame against which the output material can be assessed. The more it looks like unproblematic written-style text, the easier it should be to assimilate it into existing grammatical frameworks. From this perspective we wish to emphasise that LUG provides an essential, but hitherto largely missing, link between the superficial form of a text and the entry conditions for a range of hierarchical grammars.

Legibility

The transcript of an informal conversation requires time and effort to be easily read, because its original purpose, unlike that of ordinary written documents, is long past, and was partly shaped by a situation which is normally not recoverable. In that sense, transcripts are not very *legible*. One of the functions of LUG is to put on one side those interactive units whose main purpose is spent, and which, if they remained in linear sequence, might interfere with our observation of the incrementation of shared experience; in this way the legibility of the material is substantially increased without loss of substance.

Of the many important potential applications for the output of Step 5, one is the increase in efficiency that legibility gives to people who have to scan transcripts. Not only are there many fewer words to read, but also they are much more immediately coherent, and the reader is less likely to miss specific points. Some transcribing traditions — not linguistic ones, but legal and journalistic ones — include an editing function of this type in the original interpretation of the sound wave, using trained transcribers. While this arrangement is practical and convenient, it is dependent not only on the phonological skills of the transcribers but also on their editing skills.

Further, the science of speech recognition has made a beginning, and although it looks like slow going, we must anticipate that fully automatic transcription will eventually produce acceptable results, and with it an extraordinary torrent of transcripts. If these were passed through LUG, the legibility would be greatly improved, and the files would be available either for human perusal or for further automatic analysis. One application of this resource is that it could be of use in the espionage trade, which is reputed to be collecting by the terabyte conversations transcribed from telephones or bugged venues, or downloaded from blogs, chat rooms and other electronic sources, including text messages. An automated version of LUG could streamline the material and improve the efficiency of information extraction tools — and we will consider further possibilities of automating the analysis later in this chapter.

LUG outupt is available in analysed or plain text form. For input to an activity such as text mining, it is likely that the plain text output from LUG would be optimal, while for text summarisation, for example, the analysis should be very helpful.

Automation

There are good grounds for thinking that a large proportion of the analysis presented in this book can be automated. The primary reason for probing into this is the possibility of making the decisions less subjective, and permitting accuracy checks. However if it is successfully implemented, it will speed up analysis, allow many varieties of English to be included in corpora and open up important new areas for research and applications.

For automation, it may be best to start with Step 2 and return later to Step 1, because chunks do not come naturally to computers. However, the distinction between O and M should not be difficult in the majority of cases, because, as has been pointed out above, O items tend to follow the idiom principle and may be largely listable, with a few small sets of variants. The fact that O and M units are constructed on different principles gives a sound start to the practical matter of differentiating them. Further help comes from the frequency of O chunks, which aids the division of the text into smallish analytic categories.

We are not aware of previous work that makes use of the componential difference between O and M elements. One reason for this is perhaps that since OI elements rarely occur in normal written language, the overall frequency of O units is lower than in speech. Another reason is the convention by which conjunctions are considered to be parts of a clause, in most cases the clause which immediately follows them; it was argued in Chapter One, under the heading "Clause boundaries", that for co-ordinators at least, and sentence adverbs, this was not justified by the syntax, and it was proposed to keep OT elements separate from the surrounding clauses, at least until a good reason emerged for conflating them. No such reason has yet emerged.

Although their construction is different, there is a little overlap in realisation between O and M elements, in such phrases as *I mean, you see*, but in the general spirit of this approach to analysis, it is to be hoped that their position and their co-textual relations will keep them apart.

We return, then, to the running text, with the O elements marked off. In between them are M segments, but we do not know where relevant boundaries occur within the M segments. To model the human analysis as closely as possible, we must try to recreate the PUBs.

There are many ways of approaching this problem, and at this stage it is not possible to decide which is the best. The formal grammarians and phonologists have worked out appropriate units which can be assigned automatically — for example Abney's (1991) φ-phrases (see Chapter 2). These may be too programmatic for our purposes, and perhaps an attempt at applying at least the spirit of Catastrophe theory (see Thom 1972 and Chapter 2) will give results closer to those that people naturally achieve.

The algorithm for seeing PUBs as tiny "catastrophes" would add a weighting to each successive word as it adds itself to the growing chunk; so that, if no reductions are made, the break-point will be reached at five or maybe six words. Then there would be a prohibition on breaking up endocentric constructions; the computer would find a large proportion of these because very common words like *the* and *a/an* can only make endocentric relationships with the word that follows them.

With this tactic the programs encroach on the work of the final stage — the determination of exocentric versus endocentric relationships. Analytic information that is not determined until after Step 5 is used to help determine Step 1 boundaries. However, it is a reasonable presumption that speakers are partially guided in their boundary assignments by such matters, and therefore that it is appropriate for the software to model this aspect of their behaviour. Other encroachments are considered below, and it may be questioned whether there is any advantage in following the sequence of analytic routines that seem to work well for human beings. If exactly the same algorithms are to be used more than once on the same data, it must be justified in terms of superior results.

Against this is the argument that lies behind a lot of the design for this study — that it is very difficult to control such a complex operation as assigning grammatical structure all at once to open text, including non-standard open text. So we will at present persist with the bootstrap model of a series of simple steps, each step using whatever evidence is useful, and often re-using evidence or anticipating part of the output of a later step. At the same time we will be alert for places where some variation in tactics may give better results. It is beyond the scope of this book to do the substantial experimentation that might determine which tactic gives best results.

A second feature of English text, after the distinctiveness of the O elements, is the fact that some words are very common and occur in profusion. Making a rough distinction between common and everyday words, the two passages that we have analysed so far in this Chapter break down as follows (the O elements are excluded from these figures):

Lexis passage
Common words: *I what when you from one to the the on the* (11)
Everyday words: *wondered happens go island other train goes ferry* (8)

HKCSE passage

Common words: *with the it must be a kind of the one the other one is the it's the* (18)
Everyday words: *deep-fried pork chop butter Japanese mushroom long thin white rice roast beefs* (13)

In both these counts the apostrophe and the hyphen are considered word breaks; the number of common words is almost 60 percent of the total. So whenever a PUB is getting likely, there is also likely to be a common word close by.

The value of this evidence has already been hinted at with the incidence of the articles; there are perhaps a hundred words that occur often and are not among the major parts of speech. Conventionally they are called prepositions, determiners, conjunctions etc. but mostly their individualistic usage is more a guide to meaning than membership of these precarious word-classes.

Apart from pronouns, these words do not normally stand as textual objects; that is, they cannot be isolated with a PUB on either side, even if the relationship on either side is exocentric. This one point, if it holds up to rigorous checking, gives enormous clarification to the job of assigning the PUBs. Then each of them has a discoverable pattern of relationships which can further narrow down the options for placing PUBs. For example, to the left of *if* is placed an exocentric boundary unless the preceding word is *what, only, even* or *as*. To the right of *if* is an exocentric boundary which cannot be a PUB. So each occurrence of *if* (about once every 500 words) shines a structural light around itself, and so do the other very common words.[1]

This will amount to a lot of clarification. It has been explained that there is considerable flexibility in the assignment of PUBs, and successive stages of analysis smooth over the vagaries of individual choice in most cases; for the computer it may be more practical to express boundary assignment in terms of certain places in the alternative way suggested in Chapter 1 — to assess word-breaks as to their *un*likelihood of being PUBs rather than as their likelihood. This could resolve a great deal of the uncertainty of PUB-placement. Then a "catastrophe" program could merely avoid such places, and either skip them or stop short of them according to the weight of words in the growing segment of text since the last boundary.

Continuing, we divide O elements into OI and OT as in Step 3. In the analyses we have noted two relevant features of these items; on the one hand the actual exponents, the words and phrases, often overlap, while on the other hand their functions may not always be sharply separable—an OT element may well have a minor

---

[1]. The question of whether the very common words in English behave consistently enough to be placed in coherent word-classes is briefly addressed in Sinclair 1999).

role which is more characteristic of OI, and vice versa. In practical terms the level of accuracy needed to differentiate them will depend on the application, and in many instances it may not be very demanding; the careful argumentation presented here may not be required in the automatic version.

Next we consider how to replicate Step 4 in a program. The main criteria are the notions of *completion* and *matching*. Let us take matching first, because this is something that computers can do well; MA looks fairly straightforward, but for MR we will need fuzzy matching. However, the merging that follows the matching in groups of MR units may be one of the places where some ingenious programming is required; while as a general rule it is the last wording that is the preferred one, sometimes a composite one, including words that do not appear in the final one, is superior. In the example of MR from the HKCSE text above, the final form proposed for the MR, *a kind of Japanese mushroom* includes *a kind of*, which is not in the last two formulations of the expression.

Completion is a different matter because there is no way of telling on the surface of the text when a construction is complete, in the sense in which we are using the term (see Chapter 11). It will probably be necessary to compile a simple valency-type dictionary (Herbst et al 2005) in which are recorded patterns to be expected. Such resources in machine-usable form are called *lexicons*, and were popular some years ago in the software of Natural Language Processing, so there is a background of experience to draw on. However, before going to this sort of trouble it is necessary to assess how critical this stage is in the determination of the final result. It might perhaps be the case that with the great accuracy that can be expected from the other strategies, the distinction between +M and MS turns out not to be so important in the computer implementation.

The division into chunks mainly of two or three words brings into focus a novel resource from the large text corpora that are now available. In everyday text there is an abundance of semi-prefabricated phrases which recur with strictly limited variation, and a corpus can provide evidence of the likely syntactic relationship among the constituent words. For example, there is a chunk from the *Independent* quoted at the beginning of this chapter:

tax policy

In theory (and in any comprehensive lexicon) the word *tax* will be listed as possibly a noun or a verb. Either it modifies *policy* in an endocentric relationship, or it "governs" *policy* because *policy* is its object. A reader of this passage is in no doubt, but a computer does not know that the idea of "taxing policy" is empty or absurd. So while *tax* can occur as a verb, it does not do so in front of *policy*. A large corpus shows plenty of examples of the pair *tax policy*, invariably used as a noun phrase, and with plenty of cotextual evidence to back this up; preceding indications of a noun phrase abound, like *a common . . ., Federal . . ., our . . ., the . . .* and prepositions *in, over* and of course *of.*

It is not easy to see how this vast resource of language in use can be harnessed to sharpen automatic procedures, but to ignore it is like not noticing an elephant in the sitting room. There is great potential for a bootstrap operation, perhaps based on LUG output which has undergone the further stage outlined in this chapter.

It was emphasised in Step 5 that some of the words and phrases which are omitted in order to simplify the structure may be carrying information which should not be lost in the process of topic incrementation. Typically this information will be of a pragmatic nature, so that, for example, a string of MF elements may signal an attitude of the speaker — a lack of confidence, for example — that supports what is being said. It is not possible in this book to study the sidelined information any further, because our concentration has been on the topic increments. At this stage we suggest merely informal notes as a way of recording the information, but it is clear that there is room for a more systematic description of the information, and possibly its incorporation in an automated process. This has to be a suggestion for future research at present, a fascinating area that could take the systematic description of discourse to a new level of sophistication.

Applied Linguistics

We can anticipate uses of LUG in two important areas of applied linguistics: foreign language teaching and translation studies. In addition to its potential for raising language awareness among learners, teachers, and translators, Linear Unit Grammar can help in rethinking the shape of pedagogical grammars. In translation studies, the main benefits are likely to accrue to interpreters and interpreter education.

Language teaching

One of the big hurdles for foreign language learners is the glaring discrepancy between the grammatical rules they are taught in class and the seemingly chaotic reality of ongoing speech. With written language the gap appears narrower because written sentences tend to resemble the rules of prescription and parsing more closely than speech does, even though grammar does not take you very far in making sense of continuous text. The model we propose in this book helps bridge the gap between the linearity of language that learners hear or read and the well-formed clauses and sentences in pedagogical grammars.

Pedagogical grammars are, at best, simplifications of larger, descriptive grammars based on hierarchical models such as we have already discussed several times in this book. In reality, pedagogical grammars are rarely written by linguists (with some notable exceptions like the *Communicative Grammar of English* by Leech and

Svartvik (1975) but by practitioners who tend to carry on traditions with modifications motivated more by changing pedagogical trends than an appreciation of major linguistic developments (cf. Mauranen 2004a,b). Pedagogical grammars constitute the essence of form-focussed teaching. Focus on form has varied in popularity among the English teaching community, but is nevertheless a permanent feature in foreign language teaching (see R. Ellis 1997). Linear Unit Grammar offers an important prospect of development for pedagogical grammars by anchoring the perception of linguistic form in continuous text.

An important feature in the present model is the low level of abstraction from ongoing speech, where lexis is not separated from structure, and all aspects of language are processed simultaneously but in manageable chunks. So instead of talking about structures and lexis at different points, looking at chunks in a transcribed speech extract retains a holistic viewpoint and includes pragmatic speech management items, which usually get a rather offhand treatment in pedagogical expositions, or none at all.

This linear model of grammar makes spoken language manageable: chunking the stream of speech is natural to humans, but normally not a conscious activity. Focusing learners' attention on this ability can speed up the process of extracting meaningful information from that which is heard.

Unedited speech is typically thought to be too difficult for learners to understand before they have reached fairly advanced stages in learning the target language; scripted dialogues are favoured instead, because they presumably make relevant simplifications. This can be a problem, because the transition to language in the real world may come too late or be too abrupt to maintain students' motivation or self-confidence. Simplifications of language for pedagogical purposes are often not linguistically sufficiently well motivated or appropriately graded for helping students to achieve necessary prerequisites for dealing with the demands of the classroom-external world. They may differ markedly from the language on the whole — and from each other as well as seen in Römer's work (2005).

An alternative way of coping with unscripted speech in the early phases of learning is to take it in small doses, subject it to chunking and go through the chunks by pointing out their characteristics and discussing their roles in the discourse. A transcript is a natural way of arresting speech, because it can be combined with listening to the soundtrack and in addition it can be analysed step by step, spending as much time on explanation as is required. Like corpora of transcribed speech, the LUG approach arrests speech for pedagogical observation without interfering with the text itself (see Mauranen 2004a). Effective foreign language teaching cannot be based on merely exposing the learners to masses of authentic data; the whole point of pedagogics is to make the process of acquisition more efficient, as has convincingly been argued by Henry Widdowson on many occasions (see e.g. Widdowson

2003). However, pedagogic adaptation need not involve changing the text itself, but changing the approach: imposing a very simple model of the present kind on short extracts makes language more tractable.

When authentic language is used from the start and both O and M elements are attended to, their contributions to interaction can be noticed. This can also help raise teachers' and learners' awareness of their own speech in classroom interaction, and help alleviate the excessive interactive directness which appears to dominate current language classroom practices (see, e.g. Nikula 2002).

It is clear that most of what we have included in the present stage of our model is useful to language teachers and student teachers. As to learners themselves, the direct usefulness of the model varies depending on the maturity and level of command of the language. We maintain nevertheless that some of the procedures are useful for all learners, and all procedures are useful for some learners.

The distinction between O and M elements, as explained in Step 2 (Chapter 6) above, is particularly important for learners; if they are trying to extract message-type meanings from what they hear, they should focus their attention on these. For making sense of the main content of topic increments, it is also expedient to distinguish OI elements from OT elements (Step 3, Chapter 7), because OT contributes to the shared virtual world of interlocutors, as we saw in Step 5 (Chapter 9). Strategies of this kind are useful for working out answers to questions concerning facts: what *hazardous* means, how many percent of the population speak Turkish, why the telephone doesn't work, where the ladies' room is, etc. For certain purposes, then, it is a good idea to ignore the OI elements. However, for understanding other people's attitudes and feelings about what they are saying (*it's funny thing*), their degree of commitment or certainty (*I'm not sure*) or their reservations about what is being said (*well*), the OI elements are crucial. The different kinds of M elements (MA, M+, etc, see Chapter 8) may be less vital for many learner groups, like very young learners or students at elementary stages, but from intermediate levels onwards they are probably just as enlightening as the more basic divisions of elements.

The combination of three features of Linear Unit Grammar — the early separation of O and M units, the preservation of linearity and the "bottom up" approach to description — offer opportunities for different approaches to presenting the structure of texts. Sentence structure as we know it requires a sharp division of clauses into main and subordinate, while a linear approach would leave such a hierarchical distinction until a late stage, and might require it to be invoked only occasionally. It was pointed out in Chapter 2 that "initial" conjunctions are detachable from their following clauses because of being OTs or by extension of that distinction to include "subordinators". A linear description might suggest that O elements are like settings in process control, and the clauses themselves, when they are actually being heard or read, are all interpreted in much the same way. Concentration on written language leaves the impression that text occurs in lumps, while LUG, developed for spoken text analysis, focuses on text as a most transitory phenomenon.

Current pedagogical grammars — like most descriptive grammars — are essentially based on standard written language, and therefore do not reflect the structures of spoken language adequately (McCarthy 1998; Hughes (ed.) 2006). Our system is simple and robust enough to handle a wide variety of spoken and written texts and so bridges a good deal of the gap between speech and grammar. In this way it can reduce the alienation of grammar teaching from the practical skills of foreign language use. One of its potential uses would be as a first part of any pedagogical grammar.[2]

A more radical new departure for pedagogical grammars would be to take the present LUG as a point of departure and branch out from there into greater grammatical depths by integrating elements of existing grammars but also writing entirely new parts which have emerged in analysis but which do not usually get much coverage in pedagogical grammar. The ensuing grammar would have the advantage over most currently available pedagogical grammars that it need not be biased towards the written mode, but would be able to deal with speaking in a good balance with writing, showing differences as well as points of similarity. The treatment of O elements could incorporate much of the knowledge and research findings from discourse analysis, text linguistics and conversation analysis, which currently mostly remain outside grammars and which have some difficulty in finding a suitable niche in curricula.

It is important to integrate speaking firmly and seriously into curricula as one of the central foci of foreign language learning, not just the fun intervals between more demanding sessions. This is important in a world where foreign languages are overwhelmingly learned through the written medium, however much conversational skills are emphasised in the objectives. Moreover, the teaching of text skills, reading and writing, tend to be quite insufficiently integrated with grammar and text structure. By taking linear text as a point of departure of grammatical analysis and gradually proceeding towards greater hierarchical depth we hope to bring spoken and written text closer to grammar in a manner which is ultimately also fully adaptable to the needs of language teachers and learners.

Interpreting

LUG gives a handle on online speaking, which is what interpreters need to work with. In all interpreting, the extraction of the contributions to shared knowledge is the interpreter's main task before rendering the contribution in the target language.

---

2. This suggestion was made by Sylviane Granger in our Workshop in Ann Arbor.

At the same time, it is important for interpreters to summarise interpersonal meanings adequately. An awareness of the basic types of element, especially the distinction between O and I elements and the separation of OI from OT provides useful scaffolding for student interpreters. They need to see the relevance of both and maintain the import of both in their output; practising this can facilitate a student interpreter's acquisition of the fundamental skills of the trade.

Simultaneous interpretation stays closer to the speaker's surface expression than consecutive interpretation, but even simultaneous interpretation needs to reduce the original speech for target language rendering. The need to keep track of the gist of the topic development while keeping note of the relevant OI contributions makes consecutive interpreter' work quite taxing on memory. Practising chunking and analysing extracts of speech along the lines suggested here undoubtedly not only raises awareness of the nature of linear speech but also enables the forming of more appropriate expectations of what can lie ahead in the discourse. In other words, it can support prospection. Discarding the irrelevant and summarising the relevant elements so as to achieve the kind of normalised formulation that was demonstrated in Chapter 9 may be very helpful exercises towards acquiring fluent interpreter skills.

APPENDIX

Report from the workshop "Degenrate Data" at the joint conference of AACL and ICAME in Ann Arbor, May 11th 2005

We ran two workshops on our evolving system when we felt we had enough of interest to present to others but when the system was not fully developed; at such points feedback was very welcome to see whether our ideas were communicable, whether others found them interesting and what weak spots we had not detected ourselves. The first workshop took place in a corpus linguistics conference in Shanghai, October 2003, and gave us valuable and encouraging feedback on the method of analysis. At this stage the M units were not as yet differentiated very far. After analysing more texts of different kinds and elaborating the system further we felt the need for more feedback and offered a second workshop in a corpus linguistics conference in Michigan eighteen months later. At this stage the system was almost exactly what it is now, but the MA element type had not come up yet, and some fine-tuning was still made on the text analyses later.

The workshop thus sought to try out the system of analysis. It needs to be made clear at the outset that this does not mean testing the system in a rigorous sense, that is, it does not purport to follow any established tradition of experimental research; we have not collected exact data from the workshops, but simply kept notes of what comments we received from the participants. Nor have we at any stage subjected the system to independent raters in controlled conditions, and make no claims about inter-rater reliability. The workshops were run for the benefit of feedback and their value rests on the discussions and comments we received, not as hard evidence on the usability of the system. As we now understand our description, such attempts at control and reliability would have been misguided, because such conformity is not what we now predict.

At Ann Arbor we wanted to see how others would perform the stages of the analysis with our categories. We were also interested in how much agreement there would be, and what points would receive the most disagreement. And above all we wanted to get comments and feedback from this sophisticated audience.

We presented the analysis in a stepwise fashion so that participants had access to one step at a time. The stages corresponded to the five steps we have outlined in this book. After a brief introduction we handed out a text extract which the participants analysed. The instructions for each stage included a short sample analysis to make the task clearer. The participants worked in groups of about five, and when the groups had finished one stage, all groups were engaged in a general discussion before moving on.

We only offered a minimal and very general idea of the later steps and the final outcome of the whole exercise at the outset, simply saying that after assigning PUBs, we would go on to classify them in two stages, and then combine and reorder the units to make LUMs, which would result in a form intended to be accessible to any normal written language grammar.

For the first step, we handed out a version of the "HKCSE" text (see Chapter 10), which was presented in a word-by word form, as here:

A: yea
B: deep-fried
    pork
        chop
A: yea
B: and
    then
        with
            the
                oil
                    butter
                        um . . .

Our instructions started from the assumption that as readers (or listeners) encounter successive words and these seem to be structurally related to their predecessors, the words are held together in a provisional grouping. After a few words, the reader will encounter a pair of successive words that are perceived as not likely to belong to the same structure. We suggested that between two words of the latter kind a boundary should be placed, called a Provisional Unit Boundary (PUB).

We also pointed out that the units thus formed may be of different types, and that they might not form coherent or complete entities at this stage, and that PUB-defined units were usually very short, from one to three words, even less than a word. We emphasised focusing on the assignment of boundaries rather than paying attention on what was inside, but we advised participants to insert a boundary in cases of doubt, rather than the other way round.

The task did not seem to cause much disagreement or difficulty. Some participants said that they would have preferred a clearer indication of the size of unit desired, because interpretations will vary. True, but since we wished to tap intuitive responses, we assumed that by and large the boundaries would be similar. The assumption was borne out sufficiently for the purposes of testing the system. One boundary problem was discussed, involving what looks like an inconsistency or an arbitrary decision concerning lines 15–17 (the line numbering follows the full version in Chapter 10):

15. okay ((laugh)) okay
16. I know
17. I know

At this stage we had not yet removed the laughter indication, which we decided to do later in the interests of comparability. The question concerned the repetition of *okay* in line 15 without a boundary while 16 and 17 were separate. This could clearly be done either way, that is, the repetitions of *okay* could be separated. We left them as they were, because *I know* units were felt by many, including ourselves, to be more substantive than *okay*, but this is not a very important decision, and does not affect the final analysis into Linear Units of Meaning (LUMs).

The second step was more demanding. It involved the first classification of PUBs, and the introduction of the concepts O and M. We presented the distinction by directing attention to the elements separated by the boundaries in terms of their functions, that is, in terms of their contributions to the total communication as either updating the knowledge that emerges as shared between the participants or, alternatively, facilitating the process of updating that knowledge.

At this point we anticipated some of the potential difficulties arising from working with speech without the soundtrack. An example would be line 11, which is ambiguous in transcription because *it must be* could either be the speaker preparing for what comes up in line 12 as a conclusion, in which case it is O, or it could be the speaker actually arriving at this realisation, in which case it is an unfinished M unit.

10. B: I'm not sure
11.   it must be
12. A: kind of mushroom

The need for the soundtrack did not become a major issue at this point — instead, the difficulty of the binary choice did. We did not allow for a 'don't know' or 'indeterminate' category for the sake of the methodological principle that such a possibility tends to sweep aside difficult points if applied too early. The difficult cases are often those which give rise to the most interesting observations, and it is worth trying to find solutions to them rather than giving up on them. It is nevertheless clear that many very brief utterances which the speaker discards early are quite unclear, and it is impossible to tell whether they would have developed into an O or an M had they been continued. For the sake of simplicity, we have opted for categorising all of them as M (see Chapter 8), but this is a matter of temporary convenience and may need revision later.

In this text, points where the M categorisation can be questioned were first of all lines 8 and 9:

8. the
9. I

Both are too short to indicate how they were going to be followed; from general experience with English we might predict that *the* is relatively likely to start an M unit, while *I* could at least equally likely be the beginning of an O. This is nevertheless just speculation, there will never be any way of knowing what a speaker might have said. Thus the assignment of an M serves as a placeholder for the time being; eventually an 'indeterminate' category is required. Like 8 were also lines 18 and 31, both *the*. Line 34, *sort of*, is again hard to classify, but it is somewhat different in being an identifiable complete unit, only potentially ambiguous in terms of its function. It could indicate type, thus M, especially as it is preceded by an article, or it could indicate vagueness and speaker uncertainty, in which case it would be an O. If we maintain strict linearity to the point where the next unit is not considered for the resolution of the current unit, *sort of* and *kind of* can remain unresolvable. The criterion of a preceding article does not always work in speech, where filled pauses and indefinite articles may be very hard to tell apart. Access to sound will often help with stress placement, and the way in which the next stage in the conversation begins can make the interpretation less ambiguous. Nevertheless, we need to recognise that units of this kind can remain unresolved.

The assignment of O or M status was also raised in connection with *yea*. This appeared twice in the beginning of the extract:

1. A: yea
2. B: deep-fried pork chop
3. A: yea
4. B: and then

The point was made that this can also be an answer to a yes/no question, in which case it would be an M. Again we have a frequent item which does not unambiguously signal status on its own. It is the context that disambiguates it: without a preceding question that it might be answering, it is most likely to be an interlocutor's supportive comment, also known as backchannelling, and thus O.

A final question at this stage was raised with respect to the status of repeated items, which we see in lines 19 to 22.

19. A: the long thin white one
20. right

21. B: yes
22.   the long thin white one

It was pointed out that an interlocutor's repetition of an element is highly interactive, as it usually signals comprehension and has affiliative meaning. This point is discussed in Chapter 6 in connection with Step 2. Clearly, exchanges of this kind contribute both to the shared knowledge and to the interaction between the participants. The repeated M element does not bring anything really new to the shared knowledge, it simply confirms that this increment has been added. With the strict policy of assigning only one function to each unit, we preferred the M interpretation, because it is the M role that brings about the interactive understanding here. It is also very clear that the interactants signal mutual comprehension and cooperativeness with O elements in lines 20 and 21. It must nevertheless be pointed out that in this analysis we tend to give priority to the incremental aspects of the texts and as a result we may occasionally down-play the interactive aspects of conversation; we are aware of this and have made provision, at present informal, for relevant features of the interaction to be retained in the incremental process.

Step 3 consisted in classifying O units. The two main types were explained: OI, where the focus of the organisation is on the interaction, and OT, which focuses on the text. This step passed with practically no questions, apart from a single one which asked whether *and then* in line 4 could not be an OI. There was no support for the view, and it may have been a lapse of concentration, because this is a fairly clear instance of organising text rather than interactive relations.

Classifying M units raised more questions. We introduced all the four types we had at the time. The plain M, which was the straightforward sequence felt to be complete in itself was the clear, well-formed type. The other M units were qualified in one way or another: the incomplete MF, which was followed by a rephrase, new beginning or an O unit was to cover all the types of incompletion we have since subdivided; a +M, which links up with an MF and acts as a continuation of one, and finally a MR, which replaced a previous M unit by repeating or otherwise replacing all or part of a previous M. We further restricted the task by limiting the choice to just one M type, excluding combinations, so for instance if a unit seemed both to complete a previous unit and replace it, then +M was to take precedence over MR.

The extract begins with A saying just *yea*, and B continuing with *deep-fried pork chop*. There was a suggestion that B's utterance could well be +M, because there might be a piece of preceding discourse which it was completing. Since the extract was from an ongoing dialogue, this was a reasonable guess.

The second question concerned the analysis we presented in our key that line 5 would be an M. The alternative suggestion was that it ought to be analysed as MF, because there is no continuation to it. We took this on board and as we later subdivided the MF category, we specified this as M–.

4. B: and then
5.   with the oil
6.   butter

The final query was of the opinion that the repetition sequence in lines 13 and 14 should be read as 14 continuing 13, and thus it should be +M. This was not entirely felicitous, because what lines 13 and 14 both do is they are rephrasing A's attempt in line 12 to name the object. This activity fits best in with the category MR, which replaces a previous formulation.

12. A: kind of mushroom
13. B: it's a kind of mushroom
14. A: the Japanese mushroom

These were the comments at this stage. On the whole, Step 4 seemed to work very well: the discussion was fruitful in view of the refinements we later deemed to be necessary to cover all the different possibilities.

For the final stage, Step 5, where LUMs are formed and put together, we did not set any tasks for the workshop participants. Instead, we presented our method for doing this as a demonstration. Clearly, the steps that are required for the reconstruction (see Chapter 9) would have required another workshop session with its own stepwise instructions.

One of the general questions of principle that came up during the workshop was the status of the soundtrack in the analysis. It was suggested that this should be heard first, or that it should constitute the primary material for analysis because pausing, intonation units, and voice are important. Nobody said we should have used video material, but such a suggestion would have been in line with the demands for more naturalism. We have explained in this book already that we felt a very simple transcript would not only be a tolerable point of departure but in fact better than a full recording of the situation, because it liberates the analyst from too many simultaneous phenomena and allows the attention to concentrate on that which is to be achieved: a system of analysis which is general and simple, and which will be able to accommodate more detailed and full-blown analyses of many different kinds. We were not trying to account for all the meanings that the interlocutors were conveying and sharing (or trying but failing to share), nor were we seeking to account for the social interaction that took place. We felt that by this simple approach we had succeeded reasonably well in making an opening into little investigated but fundamental properties of language in ongoing interaction.

In all, we received very encouraging feedback for the analysis, which also pointed out more incidentally some weak spots over which we subsequently spent a good amount of time as we developed the system into its present state. In addition to the useful suggestions concerning details in the system, the fact that many participants had found it thought-provoking was important for our endeavour to continue. The emerging, though not precisely measured, consensus on the units and their classification which several participants talked about, was also encouraging. Some participants also felt that this would fit in very well with the work they were doing either with students or with computer programs, which was really welcome, because other people's perception of potential usefulness is something that analysts cannot easily foresee or manipulate.

Bibliography

Abney, S. 1991. Parsing by chunks. In *Principle-Based Parsing*, R. Berwick, S. Abney and C. Tenny (eds), 257–78. Dordrecht: Kluwer.
Aijmer, K. 1996. *Conversational Routines in English: Convention and creativity*. London: Longman.
Aijmer, K. 2002. *English Discourse Particles*. Amsterdam: John Benjamins.
Barnbrook, G. and Sinclair, J. 2001. Specialised corpus, local and functional grammars. In *Small Corpus Studies and ELT* [Studies in Corpus Linguistics 5], M. Ghadessy, A. Henry, and R. Roseberry (eds), 237–76. Amsterdam: John Benjamins.
Beaugrande, R. 1984. *Text production*. Norwood NJ: Ablex.
Becker, A.L. 1983. Towards a post-structuralist view of language learning: A short essay. *Language Learning* 33(5): 217–20.
Biber, D., Johansson, S., Leech, G., Conrad, S., and Finegan, E. 1999. *The Longman Grammar of Spoken and Written English*. London: Pearson Education.
Bloomfield, L. 1935 (1933). *Language*. London: Allen and Unwin.
Brazil, D. 1995. *A Grammar of Speech*. Oxford: Oxford University Press.
Broadbent, D., and Ladefoged, P. 1959. Auditory perception of temporal order. *Journal of the Acoustical Society of America* 31: 1539–40.
Burton, D. 1980. *Dialogue and Discourse*. London, Routledge and Kegan Paul.
Bybee, J. 2005. From usage to grammar: The mind's response to repetition. Presidential address of the LSA, 2005. http://www.unm.edu/~jbybee/Bybee%20plenary.pdf
Bybee, J. 2003. Cognitive processes in grammaticalization. In *The New Psychology of Language*, Vol. 2, M. Tomasello (ed.), 145–67. Mahwah NJ: Lawrence Erlbaum.
Bybee, J., and Hopper, P. 2001. Introduction to frequency and the emergence of linguistic structure. In *Frequency and the Emergence of Linguistic Structure*, J. Bybee and P. Hopper (eds), 1–24. Amsterdam: John Benjamins.
Carstairs-McCarthy, A. 1999. *The Origins of Complex Language*. Oxford: Oxford University Press.
Carter, R., and McCarthy, M. 2006. *Cambridge Grammar of English*. Cambridge: Cambridge University Press.
Chafe, W. 1994. *Discourse, Consciousness, and Time*. Chicago IL: University of Chicago Press.
Chafe, W. 2006. Reading aloud. In *Spoken English, TESOL and Applied Linguistics*, R. Hughes (ed.), 53–71. Basingstoke: Palgrave.
Chomsky, N. 1957. *Syntactic Structures*. The Hague: Mouton.
Chomsky, N. 1965. *Aspects of the Theory of Syntax*. Cambridge MA: MIT Press.
Coniam, D. 1998. Partial parsing: Boundary marking. *International Journal of Corpus Linguistics* 3(2): 1–21.
Couper-Kuhlen, E., and Seltin, M. 2001. Introducing interactional linguistics. In *Studies in Interactional Linguistics*, E. Couper-Kuhlen and M. Seltin (eds), 1–22. Amsterdam: John Benjamins.

Cowan, N. 2001. The magical number 4 in short-term memory: A reconsideration of mental storage capacity. *Behavioral and Brain Science* 24: 87–185.
Dąbrowska, E. 2004. *Language, Mind and Brain: Some psychological and neurological constraints on Theories of Grammar*. Edinburgh: Edinburgh University Press.
Du Bois, J. W. 2003. Discourse and Grammar In *The New Psychology of Language,* Vol. 2, M. Tomasello (ed.), 47–87. Mahwah NJ: Lawrence Erlbaum.
Ellis, N. 1996. Sequencing in SLA. Phonological memory, chunking, and points of order. *Studies in Second Language Acquisition* 18: 91–126.
Ellis, N. 2002. Frequency effects in language acquisition: A review with implications for theories of implicit and explicit language acquisition. *Studies in Second Language Acquisition* 24: 143–88.
Ellis, N. 2003. Constructions, chunking, and connectionism: The emergence of second language structure. In *The Handbook of Second Language Acquisition*, C. Doughty and M. Long (eds), 63–103. Oxford: Blackwell.
Ellis, R. 1997. *SLA Research and Language Teaching*. Oxford: Oxford University Press.
Erman, B. and Warren, B. 2000. The idiom principle and the open choice principle, *Text* 20(1): 87–120.
Esser, J. 1998. Syntactic and prosodic closure in in-line speech production. *Anglia* 116: 476–91.
Field, J. 2003. *Psycholinguistics*. London: Routledge.
Fillmore, C. J., Kay P., and O'Connor, M. 1988. Regularity and idiomaticity in grammatical constructions: The case of 'let alone'. *Language* 64(3): 501–38.
Firth, J. 1957. General linguistics and descriptive grammar. In *Papers in Linguistics 1934–195*, 216–28. Oxford: Oxford University Press.
Firth, J. 1968. A synopsis of linguistic theory, 1930–1955. In *Selected papers of J. R. Firth*, F. Palmer (ed.), 168–205. London: Longman.
Ford, C., Fox, B., and Thompson, S. 2003. Social interaction and grammar In *The New Psychology of Language*, Vol. 2, M. Tomasello (ed.), 119–43. Mahwah NJ: Lawrence Erlbaum.
Francis, W. 1963. *The English Language – An Introduction*: New York NY: Norton.
Fries, C. 1952. *The Structure of English*. New York NY: Harcourt, Brace & World.
Gee, J., and Grosjean, F. 1983. Performance structures: A psycholinguistic and linguistic appraisal. *Cognitive Psychology* 15: 411–58.
Gross, M. 1993. Local grammars and their representation by finite automata. In M. Hoey (ed.) *Data, Description, Discourse*. London: HarperCollins.
Hasegawa, T., Sekine, S., and Grishman, R. 2004. Discovering relations among named entities. In *Large Corpora. Proceedings of the annual meeting association of computational linguistics (ACL 2004)]*, 415–22. Spain: Barcelona.
Hakuta, K. 1976. A case study of a Japanese child learning English as a second language. *Language Learning* 26: 321–52.
Halford, B. 1996. *Talk Units: The structure of spoken Canadian English*. Tübingen: Narr.
Halliday, M. 1961. Categories of the theory of grammar. *Word* 17: 241–92.
Halliday, M. 1985. *An Introduction to Functional Grammar*. London: Edward Arnold.
Harris, Z. 1982. *A Grammar of English on Mathematical Principles*. New York NY: Wiley.
Herbst, T., Heath, D., Roe, I., and Götz, D. 2005. *A Valency Dictionary of English*. Berlin: Mouton de Gruyter.
Hughes, R. (ed.) 2006. *Spoken English, TESOL and Applied Linguistics*. Basingstoke: Palgrave.
Hulme, C., Roodenrys, S., Brown, G., and Mercer, R. 1995. The role of long-term memory mechanisms in memory span. *British Journal of Psychology* 86: 527–36.

Joyce, J. 1922 *Ulysses*. Paris: Shakespeare and Company.
Kempson, R., Meyer-Viol, W., and Gabbay, D. 2001. *Dynamic Syntax: The flow of language understanding*. London: Blackwell.
Krishnamurthy, R. (ed) 2004. *English Collocational Studies* (Republication of J. Sinclair, S. Jones and R. Daley, 1970, *English Lexical Studies*). London: Continuum.
Kurhila, S. 2003. *Co-constructing Understanding in Second Language Conversation*. Helsinki: University of Helsinki.
Laury, R. 2006. Miten vaikeasta tulee helppoa – kompleksisten lauseyhdistelmien tuottaminen keskustelussa. In *Kohtauspaikkana kieli. Näkökulmia persoonaan, muutoksiin ja valintoihin*, T. Nordlund, T. Onikki-Rantajääskö and T. Suutari (eds), 200–13. Helsinki: SKS.
Leech, G., and Svartvik, J. 1975. *A Communicative Grammar of English*. London: Longman.
Lerner, G. 1991. On the syntax of sentences in progress. *Language in Society* 20(3): 441–58.
Levelt, W. 1989. *Speaking*. Cambridge MA: MIT Press.
Mauranen, A. 2004a. Spoken corpus for an ordinary learner. In *How to Use Corpora in Language Teaching*, J. Sinclair (ed.), 89–105. Amsterdam: John Benjamins.
Mauranen, A. 2004b. Speech corpora in the classroom. In *Corpora and Language Learners*, G. Aston, S. Bernardini, and D. Stewart (eds), 197–213. Amsterdam: John Benjamins.
Mauranen, A. 2006. Signalling and preventing misunderstanding in English as lingua franca communication. *International Journal of the Sociology of Language* 177: 123–50.
Mauranen, A. Forthcoming a. Spoken rhetoric: How do natives and non-natives fare? In *Proceedings of the Conference on Cross-linguistic and Cross-Cultural Perspectives on Academic Discourse*, Suomela-Salmi, E. (ed). Turku: Turku University Press.
Mauranen, A. Forthcoming b. Hybrid voices: English as a lingua franca of academics. In K. Flottum and and T. Dahl (eds), *Academic Voices in Contrast*. Cambridge: Cambridge Scholars Press.
Mazeland, H., and Huiskes, M. 2001. Dutch 'but' as a sequential conjunction. In *Studies in Interactional Linguistics*, M. Selting and E. Couper-Kuhlen (eds), 141–69. Amsterdam: John Benjamins.
McCarthy, M. 1998. *Spoken Language and Applied Linguistics*. Cambridge: Cambridge University Press.
McCarthy, M., and Carter, R. 1997. Grammar, tails and affect: Constructing expressive choices in discourse. *Text* 17(3): 405–29.
McLaughlin, B. 1987. *Theories of Second-Language Learning*. London: Edward Arnold.
Miller, G. 1956. The magical number seven, plus or minus two: Some limits on our capacity for processing information. *Psychological Review* 63: 81–97.
Mukherjee, J. 2001. *Form and Function of Parasyntactic Presentation Structures. A corpus-based study of talk units in spoken English*. Amsterdam: Rodopi.
Mulder, J. 1989. *Foundations of Axiomatic Functionalism*. Berlin: Mouton de Gruyter.
Nattinger, J., and DeCarrico, J. 1992. *Lexical Phrases and Language Teaching*. Oxford: Oxford University Press.
Neisser, U. 1980. *Cognition and Reality: Principles and implications of cognitive psychology*. San Francisco CA: W. H. Freeman.
Nida, E. 1960. *A Synopsis of English Syntax* [SIL series 4] Norman OK; University of Oklahoma.
Nikula, T. 2002. Teacher talk reflecting pragmatic awareness: A look at EFL and content-based classrooms. *Pragmatics* 12(4): 447–67.

O'Grady, W. 2005. *Syntactic Carpentry. An emergentist approach to syntax*. Mahwah NJ: Lawrence Erlbaum.

Östman, J. O. and Fried, M. (eds) 2005. *Construction Grammars. Cognitive grounding and theoretical extensions*. Amsterdam: John Benjamins.

Palmer, H. E. 1924. *A Grammar of Spoken English on a Strictly Phonetic Basis*. Cambridge: Heffer.

Paradis, M. 2004. *A Neurolinguistic Theory of Bilingualism*. Amsterdam: John Benjamins.

Pawley, A. and Syder F. 1983. Two puzzles for linguistic theory: Nativelike selection and nativelike fluency. In *Language and Communication,* J. Richards, and R. Schmidt (eds), 191–226. New York NY: Longman.

Rumelhart, D. 1980. Schemata: The building blocks of cognition. In *Theoretical Issues in Reading Comprehension*, R. Spiro, B. Bruce and W. Brewer (eds), 33–58. Hillsdale NJ: Lawrence Erlbaum.

Römer, U. 2005. *Progressives, Patterns, Pedagogy*. Amsterdam: John Benjamins.

Rühlemann, C. 2006. Coming to terms with conversational grammar: Dislocation and dysfluency. *International Journal of Corpus Linguistics* 11(4):

Schegloff, E., and Sacks, H. 1973. Opening up closings *Semiotica* VIII(4): 290–327.

Schegloff, E., Ochs, E., and Thompson, S. 1996. Introduction. In *Interaction and Grammar*, E. Ochs, E. Schegloff, and S. Thompson (eds), 1–51. Cambridge: Cambridge University Press.

Selkirk, E. 1984. *Phonology and Syntax: The relation between sound and structure*. Cambridge MA: MIT Press.

Selting, M. and Couper-Kuhlen, E. (eds) 2001. *Studies in Interactional Linguistics* [Studies in Discourse and Grammar 10]. Amsterdam: John Benjamins.

Sinclair, J. 1972a. *A Course in Spoken English: Grammar*. Oxford: Oxford University Press.

Sinclair, J. 1972b. Lines about Lines. In *Current Trends in Stylistics*, B. Kachru, B. Stahlke, and F. Herbert (eds), 251–61. Edmonton: Linguistic Research Inc. (Reprinted in *Language and Literature* R. Carter (ed.) 1982, 163–76. London: Allen & Unwin).

Sinclair, J. 1982. Planes of discourse. In *The Two-fold Voice: Essays in honour of Ramesh Mohan*, S. Rizvil (ed.), 70–91. India: Pitambar.

Sinclair, J. 1988. Compressed English. In *Varieties of Written English*, M. Ghadessy (ed), 130–6. London: Pinter.

Sinclair, J. 1991. *Corpus Concordance Collocation*. Oxford: Oxford University Press.

Sinclair, J. 1993. Written discourse structure. In *Techniques of Description: Spoken and written discourse: A Festschrift for Malcolm Coulthard*, J. Sinclair, M. Hoey, and G. Fox (eds), 6–31. London: Routledge.

Sinclair, J. 1999. A way with common words. In *Out of Corpora: Studies in honour of Stig Johansson*, H. Hasselgård and S. Oksefjell (eds), 157–79. Amsterdam: Rodopi

Sinclair, J. 2004. The search for units of meaning in *Trust the Text*, 24–48. London: Routledge.

Sinclair, J. Forthcoming 2007. The exploitation of meaning: Literary text and local grammars. In *PALA Papers 2: Challenging the Boundaries*. I. Bas and D. Freeman (eds). Amsterdam: Rodopi.

Sinclair, J., and Coulthard R. 1975. *Towards an Analysis of Discourse*. Oxford: Oxford University Press.

Smith, F. 1978. *Understanding Reading* (2nd ed.). New York NY: Holt, Rinehart and Winston.

Stenström, A. B. 1994. *An Introduction to Spoken Interaction*. London: Longman.

Tadros, A. 1985. *Prediction in Text* [Discourse Analysis Monographs 10]. Birmingham: ELR, University of Birmingham.
Thom, R. 1972. *Structural Stability and Morphogenesis*. Boulder CO: Westview Press.
Widdowson, H. 2003. *Defining Issues in Applied Linguistics*. Oxford: Oxford University Press.
Stubbs, M. 1996. *Text and Corpus Analysis*. Oxford: Blackwell.
Wong Fillmore, L. 1979. Individual differences in second language acquisition. In *Individual Differences in Language Ability and Language Behavior,* C. J. Fillmore, D. Kempler and W. S.-Y. Wang (eds), 203–28. New York NY: Academic Press.
Wray, A. 2002. *Formulaic Language and the Lexicon*. Cambridge: Cambridge University Press.
Yang, H. J. 1986. A new technique for identifying scientific/technical terms and describing science texts. *Literary and Linguistic Computing* 1(2): 93–103.

http://www.fun-with-words.com/ambiguous_garden_path.html
http://en.wikipedia.org/wiki/Chunking_(psychology)
http://www.cnts.ua.ac.be/conll2000/chunking/

Primary sources:
ELFA: http://www.uta.fi/laitokset/kielet/engf/research/elfa/
Joyce, James 1922 Ulysses; Paris, Shakespeare and Company. Electronic version http://ccat.sas.upenn.edu/jod/ulysses.html
LEXIS: http://ota.ahds.ac.uk/texts/0173.html
MICASE: http://www.hti.umich.edu/m/micase/
Pears Cyclopedia, 94th edition 1985: Feltham Books Ltd.
The Independent, July 19, 2005.

Index of names

A
Abney 26, 159
Aijmer 29
Aijmer 75

B
Bar-Hillel 23
Barnbrook 26, 148
Beaugrande 30
Becker 9, 40
Biber 29, 81
Bloomfield 148
Brazil viii, 27ff., 36, 132, 143,
Broadbent 31
Burton 123
Bybee 34, 38, 39

C
Carstairs-McCarthy 29, 30
Carter 81
Chafe 35
Cheng 117
Chomsky 23, 135, 136ff.
Coniam 26
Coulthard 29, 129,
Couper-Kuhlen 38, 83
Cowan 35

D
Dąbrowska 37
DeCarrico 40
Du Bois 38

E
Ellis, N. 34, 39, 40
Ellis, R. 163
Erman 39

F
Field 81
Fillmore 40

Firth 150, 151
Ford 38, 81
Francis 25
Fried 31, 40
Fries 23

G
Gee 26
Granger 165n
Grosjean 26
Gross 26

H
Hakuta 40
Halford 36
Halliday 14, 28, 60, 156
Harris 137
Harris 23
Hasegawa 26
Herbst 161
Hopper 34
Hughes 165
Huiskes 77
Hulme 35

J
Johansson 29n

K
Kempson 32ff.
Kurhila 114

L
Ladefoged 31
Laury 38
Leech 162
Lerner 73
Levelt 37, 81

M
Mauranen 81, 114

Mazeland 77
McCarthy 81, 165
MICASE 136n, 138n
Miller 31, 34, 37, 131
Mukherjee 34, 38
Mulder 36

N
Nattinger 40
Neisser 37
Nida 23ff., 148
Nikula 164

O
O'Grady 32ff.
Östman 31, 40

P
Paradis 35
Pike 23
Porter 140n

R
Römer 163
Rumelhart 37

S
Saussure 133
Schegloff 38
Selkirk 26
Seltin 38
Selting 83
Smith 37
Stenström 75
Strawson 29/30
Stubbs 39
Svartvik 163

T
Tadros 100
Thom 131, 159

W
Warren 39, 117
Wells 23
Widdowson 163
Wong Fillmore 39, 40
Wray 34, 39, 81

Y
Yang 26

Index of subjects

A
action-oriented 155
additional 155
alphanumeric 49
alternation 132
analysis, sample texts 107ff.
Applied Linguistics 162
attribute-value 125
automation of analysis 158
autonomous plane 60

B
backchannelling 114, 117
bootstrap model 159
bottom up 9
boundary xvii, 12ff., 55ff.
bracketing 153

C
catastrophes 131, 159
chunk xvi, xx, 3, 6, 12ff., 26ff., 51, 55ff., 130, 163
chunking 3, 6–7, 16ff., 97, 116, 131ff., 163, 166
clause 13, 76
coherence 98
collaboration 129, 135,
  collaborative completion 73
  collaborative discourse 140
combinations 86ff.
comments, sample texts 107ff.
competition 129
completion, completive 11, 15, 83, 136ff., 161
componence 133ff.
compression 44
conjunct 75
context of situation 150
Conversation Analysis 73
conversation 60, 78, 108
core status 155

cotext 134,
cyclical analysis xviii

D
Degenrate Data 168
delicacy 8
discourse analysis 73, 129
discourse particle 3, 75
disjunct 75

E
editorial 117ff.
elements xx, 51
  +M– 84, 86
  +M 83
  M– 82
  M xxi, 59ff., 71
  MA 84
  MF 80
  MR 85ff.
  MS 84ff.
  O xxi, 59ff., 71
  OI xxi, 72
  OT xxi, 72
ELFA text *see* texts
ellipsis 150
endocentric 148, 151ff.
exclusion 143
exhaustive 52
exocentric 148, 151ff.
explicitness 49
extracts 41

F
finished 136ff.
focus 155
free indirect speech 122

G
garden path 11
Gazetteer text 44

grammar xvi, xviii, 54, 75, 78, 103, 134,
  abstract 141
  pedagogical 162
  received 142
  regular 146

H
head 79
hedge 68
hierarchy xv, 5, 142
HKCSE text *see* texts
holistic 163

I
ideational metafunction 60
idiom principle 148
if clauses 88
inclusion 143
incomplete data 61
incomplete M 82
increment 15ff., 28, 51, 59, 63, 65ff., 79
Independent text *see* texts
information science 156ff.
insubstantial 155
interactive 19, 64, 71, 103
  organisation 78
  plane 68
interpenetration 156
interpreting 165ff.
intuition 50

J
Joyce text *see* texts

L
language teaching 162
laughter 43
left dislocation 79
legibility 157

lexicons 161
Lexis text *see* texts
linear expectations 155ff.
Linear Unit Grammar xv, xix,
    32, 134, 142ff., 146ff.
  summary 154–6
  applications 156–66
Linear Unit of Meaning xx, 54,
    154, 169
linear xviii, 5, 27, 30, 37, 132
linearity 142
literary text 120
local grammar 143, 148
LUG xv, xix, 32, 134, 142ff., 146ff.
LUM xx, 54, 154, 169

M element xxi, 59ff., 71
  M– 82
  +M– 84
  +M 83
  MA 84
  MF 80, 87
  MR 85ff.
  MS– 87
  MS 84ff.
matches
  rhetorical 139
  structural 139
  subliminal 139
matching 138, 161
message x, 51
  adjustment 84
  fragment 80
  revision 85ff.
  supplement 84ff.
message-oriented 79, 119, 155
  element 60

N
narrative 62, 109
narrator 109
Natural Language
    Processing 161
negotiating the referent 79
negotiating topic 79
nominal structures 80

O
O element xxi, 59ff., 71
  OI xxi, 72
  OT element xxi, 72, 154
open-choice principle 148
order 71ff.,
organisational 51
organisation-oriented
    element 60, 133,
orientation 155
originator 141
overlapping 156

P
paradigmatic 6, 133ff., 156
paragraph structure 124
partial parser 147
participant 140, 141
pausing 80ff.
pedagogical grammars 162
pejorative 4
preprocessing 50
prescriptivism 143
prospected 156
prospecting 155
prospection 135
Provisional Unit Boundary xx,
    51, 159ff., 168
PUB xx, 51, 159ff., 168

Q
qualified status 155

R
recipient 141
recurrence 139
regimentation 98
repeats 80ff.
robustness 41

S
sampling 41
sentence adverb 76
sentence 138
separate 156
shallow parser 147
shared experience 79, 150

shared knowledge 59ff., 66
short term memory 31, 34, 37
  see also working memory
single cycle 142, 145
situation-focused 155
soundtrack 114, 172
spoken data 4, 41
status 155
step by step 50
stream of consciousness 69, 122
substantial 155
substantialness 155
suspension of disbelief 76
syntagmatic xviii, 156
syntagmatic axis 133ff.
  relations 148
synthesis 91ff.
  summary 96
system network 156

T
taxonomic 14
text mining 158
text xvi, xx
text-focused 155
texts
  analysis 107ff.
  comments 107ff.
  ELFA 42, 57, 67ff., 74ff., 99,
      110ff.
  Gazetteer 44, 123ff.
  HKCSE 43, 51, 61, 66ff., 76,
      115ff., 154, 160, 168
  Independent 43, 57ff., 64,
      117ff.
  Joyce 44, 68ff., 76ff., 120ff.
  Lexis 42, 55, 62ff., 72, 107ff.
      151, 160
textual incident 149, 154
textual object 149
textual organisation 78
textual organiser 154
top down 9
topic 59ff., 79
  topic increment 133, 150
turns 113
  long 113

U
unexpected 156

V
variety xv, 3
virtual world 150

W
well-formedness 137
working memory 131,
written data 4, 41, 64

In the series *Studies in Corpus Linguistics (SCL)* the following titles have been published thus far or are scheduled for publication:

27 **SCHNEIDER, Stefan:** Reduced Parenthetical Clauses. A corpus study of spoken French, Italian and Spanish. xiii, 238 pp. *Expected January 2007*
26 **JOHANSSON, Stig:** Seeing through Multilingual Corpora. On the use of corpora in contrastive studies. *Expected January 2007*
25 **SINCLAIR, John McH. and Anna MAURANEN:** Linear Unit Grammar. Integrating speech and writing. 2006. xxi, 185 pp.
24 **ÄDEL, Annelie:** Metadiscourse in L1 and L2 English. 2006. x, 243 pp.
23 **BIBER, Douglas:** University Language. A corpus-based study of spoken and written registers. 2006. viii, 261 pp.
22 **SCOTT, Mike and Christopher TRIBBLE:** Textual Patterns. Key words and corpus analysis in language education. 2006. x, 203 pp.
21 **GAVIOLI, Laura:** Exploring Corpora for ESP Learning. 2005. xi, 176 pp.
20 **MAHLBERG, Michaela:** English General Nouns. A corpus theoretical approach. 2005. x, 206 pp.
19 **TOGNINI-BONELLI, Elena and Gabriella DEL LUNGO CAMICIOTTI (eds.):** Strategies in Academic Discourse. 2005. xii, 212 pp.
18 **RÖMER, Ute:** Progressives, Patterns, Pedagogy. A corpus-driven approach to English progressive forms, functions, contexts and didactics. 2005. xiv + 328 pp.
17 **ASTON, Guy, Silvia BERNARDINI and Dominic STEWART (eds.):** Corpora and Language Learners. 2004. vi, 312 pp.
16 **CONNOR, Ulla and Thomas A. UPTON (eds.):** Discourse in the Professions. Perspectives from corpus linguistics. 2004. vi, 334 pp.
15 **CRESTI, Emanuela and Massimo MONEGLIA (eds.):** C-ORAL-ROM. Integrated Reference Corpora for Spoken Romance Languages. 2005. xviii, 304 pp. (incl. DVD).
14 **NESSELHAUF, Nadja:** Collocations in a Learner Corpus. 2005. xii, 332 pp.
13 **LINDQUIST, Hans and Christian MAIR (eds.):** Corpus Approaches to Grammaticalization in English. 2004. xiv, 265 pp.
12 **SINCLAIR, John McH. (ed.):** How to Use Corpora in Language Teaching. 2004. viii, 308 pp.
11 **BARNBROOK, Geoff:** Defining Language. A local grammar of definition sentences. 2002. xvi, 281 pp.
10 **AIJMER, Karin:** English Discourse Particles. Evidence from a corpus. 2002. xvi, 299 pp.
9   **REPPEN, Randi, Susan M. FITZMAURICE and Douglas BIBER (eds.):** Using Corpora to Explore Linguistic Variation. 2002. xii, 275 pp.
8   **STENSTRÖM, Anna-Brita, Gisle ANDERSEN and Ingrid Kristine HASUND:** Trends in Teenage Talk. Corpus compilation, analysis and findings. 2002. xii, 229 pp.
7   **ALTENBERG, Bengt and Sylviane GRANGER (eds.):** Lexis in Contrast. Corpus-based approaches. 2002. x, 339 pp.
6   **TOGNINI-BONELLI, Elena:** Corpus Linguistics at Work. 2001. xii, 224 pp.
5   **GHADESSY, Mohsen, Alex HENRY and Robert L. ROSEBERRY (eds.):** Small Corpus Studies and ELT. Theory and practice. 2001. xxiv, 420 pp.
4   **HUNSTON, Susan and Gill FRANCIS:** Pattern Grammar. A corpus-driven approach to the lexical grammar of English. 2000. xiv, 288 pp.
3   **BOTLEY, Simon Philip and Tony McENERY (eds.):** Corpus-based and Computational Approaches to Discourse Anaphora. 2000. vi, 258 pp.
2   **PARTINGTON, Alan:** Patterns and Meanings. Using corpora for English language research and teaching. 1998. x, 158 pp.
1   **PEARSON, Jennifer:** Terms in Context. 1998. xii, 246 pp.